Collecting More Household Linens

With Values

Frances
Johnson

Schiffer Publishing Ltd

77 Lower Valley Road, Atglen, PA 19310

D1567867

Lace tablecloths, like this one, were very popular in the
forties and fifties. $25-$35.

Copyright © 1997 by Frances Johnson
Library of Congress Catalog Card Number: 97-65379

Printed in China
ISBN: 0-7643-0208-6

Book Design by Laurie A. Smucker

Published by Schiffer Publishing Ltd.
4880 Lower Valley Road
Atglen, PA 19310
Phone: (610) 593-1777; Fax: (610) 593-2002
E-mail:Schifferbk@aol.com
Please write for a free catalog.
This book may be purchased from the publisher.
Please include $2.95 for shipping.
Try your bookstore first.

We are interested in hearing from authors
with book ideas on related subjects.

Contents

Chapter One
Fabrics, Factory-Made

When fabric was being made at home the names were simple, descriptive ones like wool, linen, cotton, silk, and linsey-woolsey—a combination of wool yarn and linen thread. But factory-made fabric was another matter altogether. As there has always been, there was competition among the manufacturers with each wanting his share of the business—or more. The only way he knew to get it was to use fancy, exciting names and maybe lower the price a few cents a yard.

Probably one of the most popular, factory-made fabrics was ticking. It was used over a longer period of time and was a necessity for every family, as it was used to make the "ticking" for feather beds. Feather beds were absolutely essential for every family, and there was a time when the ability of the housewife was judged by the number of feather beds she owned. Since they didn't cost anything in monetary terms, except for the ticking, only a willingness to work, there was no reason one could not have dozens of feather beds with matching feather pillows. The most popular type of ticking and the least expensive was the blue and white striped that came in widths of 27, 30, and 36 inches with the 30 inch being the most popular. The 36 inch was sewn together in the middle to form the ticking for the feather beds. The other sizes were used for pillows. Later an art ticking would be made. It was usually bought and used by the more affluent housewives because it was just a bit more expensive and certainly more luxurious. It usually came in stripes of green, pink, or light blue, and might also include a small floral print.

For centuries women did all kinds of needlework, some making items that were absolutely necessary for use in their homes and others making the beautiful things just to add elegance and charm to their surroundings. Not only did they weave beautiful coverlets, they made linsey-woolsey sheets with the added personal touch of embroidery across the top and bottom. They wove wool blankets with colored stripes on the top and bottom. Some then embroidered their initials and a border along the top. One of the most beautiful bedspreads, we think, is one shown in the chapter on bedspreads. It a woven, wool embroidered in wool yarn. Apparently there wasn't an abundance of colors to dye the yarn as only four were used.

As more and more factory-made fabrics became available, those who could afford it became very picky about the type of fabric they used for their household linens. Linen was one of the all-time favorites. If there is any question about that, check any or all of the old linens offered for sale now. There will be many types, and when these pieces were made there were a lot of trade names, but in the end they were all linen. Prob-

ably one of the most popular types was one called Embroidery or Art linen. It seems this type could be made any way the women wanted, as old advertisements describe it as either a close or loose weave, or it could be unbleached, quarter bleached, half bleached, or white. This statement alone explains why it is so difficult now for us to determine exactly what type was used a century ago. With the many washings this fabric has had through the years, even the unbleached has now turned white. Another fabric was called Cambric linen and was described as best for making church embroidery, lunch cloths, napkins, and doilies.

Damask is the name of a fabric that was named for the ancient city of Damascus. Later the name became synonymous with table linens, probably due to the fact that our grandmothers felt the dining room table had to be covered in a snowy white damask tablecloth. She might have dozens of these cloths because she believed in changing them regularly—and it wasn't only the tablecloths. Most families had stacks of napkins that matched the cloths. Napkins came in a variety of sizes, but the choice ones were 20 to 24 inches square and hemmed by hand. These were saved for special family dinners or parties. Although the damask had a light woven-in design, nevertheless the women added more, usually satin stitched monograms.

Huck, huckaback, and just plain toweling are some of the names given to the fabric used to make towels. Handmade towels were an important part of the early household as not only were dish towels handmade, and often embroidered, but hand towels were a very important item in early households. One of the reasons for this was because not all homes at that time had bathrooms. Instead there was a washstand with a bowl and pitcher set in every bedroom. Family and guests alike dressed in their bedroom after first taking a bath of sort using water in the bowl. Towels were provided for each guest, along with a splasher for the washstand. The splasher was hung over the rod on the top of the washstand to prevent water from splashing on the wallpaper behind it. The term huckaback comes from the English where the foot peddlers were called hucksters. Since they carried their wares on his backs, the two words were combined to form the name of a fabric used to make towels. Oftentimes borders, sometimes fancy, other times plain, were woven on one or both ends of the towel. Other trade names for fabrics that were used for toweling included crash, birdseye, damask, honeycomb, twill, and Turkish.

This may come as a surprise to some, but ready-made sheets only came into general use during the last quarter century. Prior to that time most farm families and many who lived in the small towns and villages made their own sheets using sheeting or muslin, the latter named for the ancient city of Mosul where this particular fabric was first made. This fabric could be bought bleached or unbleached. It was a firm, plain white (when bleached) cotton fabric that was most often described as stronger and heavier than longcloth. In the very early days in this country fabric for sheets was made by weaving a combination of wool yarn and flax thread. They called it linsey-woolsey. Through the years both sheets and pillow cases have been made of linen. Pillow tubing was also made and sold during those years. It might be plain or with a design, and was always made so that it was very easy to simply cut and seam up.

Another fabric that became extremely popular during the early part of this century were grain and feed sacks. At first they were simply heavy, white cotton bags filled with grain and sold to the farmer to feed his livestock in winter. Since people were still in that "Waste Not-Want Not" era, they used the fabric from the sacks to an advantage. Once the grain or feed had been used, they washed the bags and raveled out the thread used to stitch up the bottom and sides. The bags were then used to make sheets, bedspreads, and even work shirts. The thread that had been used to sew up the bag was used to make crochet or tatting for pillow cases. One man told a story about his grandmother paying him 5 cents a yard to tat the thread into a coarse lace for use on both sheets and pillow cases. For about twenty-five years, beginning in the 1930s, the manufacturers of fabric to be used for making feed and grain bags began making it with pretty figured designs. This fabric then served another purpose—it began to be used to make girl's dresses, pillow cases, aprons, and if the design was suitable, into boy's shirts. These old feed sacks are again becoming popular.

As we study fabrics there are many expressions that raise questions, such as why and how did it begin. Turkey red is an example. Well, it seems this bright red was once made from madder dye brought from Turkey. The term "in the grease" refers to wool just as it has been sheared from the sheep, before it has been scrubbed. "In the gum" is a phrase used in silk culture. It refers to silk in its raw or natural state, that is, before it is degummed. At that time it contained sericin or silk gum which made it dull and stiff. "In the gray" refers to unbleached or undyed cotton or linen fabric. And finally there is the word Shoddy, a name used to describe fabric made from the rough, left-over wool, or that made by shredding woolen or worsted fabric and re-using it to make yarn and fabric.

But to better understand the rising popularity of factory-made fabrics we only have to study the progress of one mill—Bates Manufacturing Company, Lewiston, Maine. This mill kept such good records it is easy to check them and get an idea how they all worked. The mill opened in late 1850 with 200 workers. The monthly payroll was $3,900 which gives an idea of salaries for each person. That first year their total sales were only $19,308.81, a piddling amount by today's standards. But the demand for factory made fabrics was increasing almost daily. It was common knowledge among new mill owners in 1850 that 98 percent of the fabric made in America was made in the home and used by the family that made it. This trend was changing because records show that by 1857 Bates had 3,600 spindles running, was employing 1,000 people, and making 5,700,000 yards of fabric a year. During the Civil War years Bates became quite famous for their duck fabric, used for making tents. By 1870 Bates was making over a million and a half bags a year as wells as six million yards of fabric. The fabrics they were making included plaids, twills, fancy checks, shirting stripes, fancy and heavy cassimeres, towels, batting, twills, gambroons, denims, and jeans. A decade later they were also making shoe cloth, toweling, chevoits, piques, tape, horse covers, corset cloth, cotton blankets, checked tablecloths, curtain cloth, hammock cloth, seersucker, shirtings, and diapers.

Factory-made, multi-colored gingham.

Multi-colored, factory-made fabric with different check.

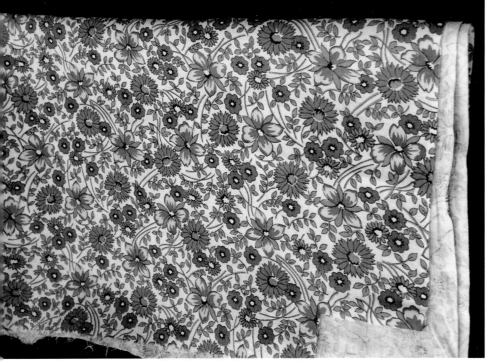

Empty, floral, feed and grain bags like these were used by farm families to make clothing and pillow cases in the thirties and forties.

Women who couldn't or didn't want to add needlework to their household linens often used figured fabric like this.

Checkered damask for tablecloths.

In the forties and fifties fabric featuring people, animals, and trees were used to make trapunto pictures. The process was a type of quilting that created a raised effect by outlining the designs with a running stitch, then stuffing it with cotton.

Feed or grain bag with different design.

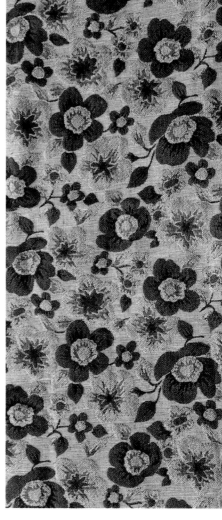

Figured, factory-made fabric like this could be used for making small tablecloths as well as pillow cases.

Until the feathers were removed recently this blue and white ticking was a feather bed.

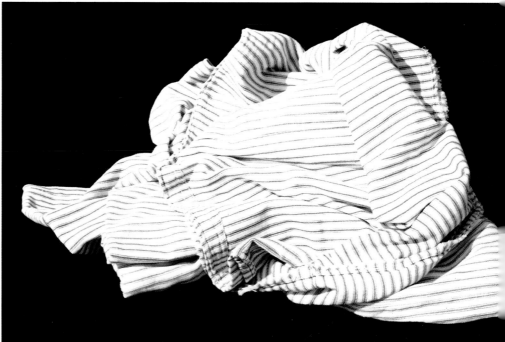

Heavily woven fabric like this was used for draperies and upholstery in the forties through the seventies.

Another favorite drapery and upholstery fabric from the forties to the seventies period.

Old sewing machines like this were used earlier, and some continued to be used well into the sixties.

Another old sewing machine.

Chapter Two
Types of Fabrics

A variety of factory-made fabrics can still be found today, but nothing to compare with what was available half a century ago. At that time people depended more on making their own clothing than on buying ready made. Most women were expert seamstresses and the few who weren't had a relative who sewed for them, or a paid seamstress. So for that reason there were bolts and bolts of fabric available in everything from the little hole-in-the-wall fabric store to the large dry goods stores. It would be difficult today for young people to even imagine what those large dry goods stores were like. It was a different time and customs were different then. Even as late as the fifties and sixties women still went shopping, and it was shopping, not just running by the store to pick up something she needed. At that time women dressed to go shopping, that is they wore hats and gloves along with their best suits or dresses. They might spend the whole day and have lunch with their husband or with friends. The least time they might spend on one of these shopping excursions would be a long afternoon. They seldom took the children with them except on special occasions when the child had to have new shoes and they needed to be fitted. If there was more than one child in the family, the children were taken shopping one at a time while the remainder of the children were left home with a relative or the maid. This made the trip special for the child and the mother could concentrate on that child's needs.

This writer remembers well one of her early shopping trips with her mother. I was about eight to ten years old and my mother had decided I was old enough to pick out the fabric for my school dresses, the dresses my mother would either make or let a visiting seamstress cousin make when she arrived for her annual visit. In our family and others like us in the rural areas of the south, poor, widowed relatives came for long visits and did many chores for which they were paid, room, board, and some money. These relatives were usually skilled in some types of work, such as sewing or carpentry, and this arrangement worked out well for both parties. But back to our shopping trip. We went to the largest dry goods store in our town. Even today the memory of those shelves filled with hundreds of bolts of fabric is mind boggling. The shelves, approximately 10 to 12 feet tall and 20 to 25 feet wide were filled completely with bolts of fabric. In front of the shelves was a smooth counter with yard sticks nailed down for measuring the fabric. Three or four clerks might be working around this counter at all times, depending on the number of customers. After the customer had made a choice the clerk unwound the bolt and measured the fabric on the yard stick. And as sort of an early southern lagniappe (a small

gift for a good customer) the clerk would move her finger and thumb over about two inches at the end of the yardstick. Each time she measured another yard she added another couple of inches. If the customer had calculated closely, this would assure her she would have enough to cut the garment easily. I still remember one of the choices we made that day. It was a tiny lavender-checked gingham and one of the softest pieces of gingham I thought I'd ever seen. Probably one of the reasons I remember it so well is the fact I knew we wouldn't get that one when I saw the 10 cents a yard price tag on the end of the bolt. Regular gingham was only 5 to about 8 cents a yard and with several girls to buy for my mother had to watch every penny. Apparently she saw the disappointment on my face and whispered that she liked my choice—and I could have it. I wore that dress until it was in tatters.

It wasn't only the amount of fabric in those days that was impressive, it was also the names. It would be extremely difficult today for us to even remember those names and to try to identify each by name would be close to impossible. In an effort to help collectors who want to try to identify their pieces, we have assembled a list of names used in various books, catalogues, and magazines, fabrics that were recommended for household linens.

The first is Ada Canvas. It could be found in both linen and cotton, usually tan in color, and was especially adaptable to cross stitch. Another was Art Linen or Embroidery Linen, a term that was said to describe a variety of crashes. That is not very helpful today when so many people are not familiar with crashes. But at the time it was highly recommended for luncheon cloths, napkins, and runners. One fabric that is easier to recognize is Canton linen also called grass cloth, Chinese grass cloth, and plain old grass linen. It was so named because it was made of ramie also known as China grass. Although the threads are heavier in your ramie sweaters it will give you an idea of the texture. Damask is one of the easiest to identify, as everybody's grandmother had damask tablecloths. In fact, it became so well known that the terms damask and tablecloth were used together more often than they were used singularly. Identifying damask is easy, but deciding whether it is single damask or double damask takes a little time. It is easy when you remember the single type is just what the name implies—a thin, light fabric. Double damask is the opposite—a good, heavily woven fabric.

Many fabrics were named for the use for which they were made. One example is glass toweling. It probably had another name at the factory, but the ladies asked for glass toweling in the stores. It might be all white or white with colored borders. Its claim to fame was the fact it could be used to dry glassware and would not leave lint. Honeycomb or waffle cloth was another type of toweling that was very popular with the ladies in the early part of this century. This was more a type of toweling than a brand name. The uneven, soft surface allowed more absorption than a smooth surface. Huck or huckaback is another type of toweling that was made of cotton, union (a fabric made of two fibers), or linen. It could have either a small design or a damask figure, and it might be woven in towel lengths with a border on either end. The borders could be either all-white or in colors with the name of a hotel or railroad woven into them. These towels can still be found today indicating they weren't used as much as expected—or maybe they were just being saved as some of them are quite collectible today, especially those from defunct railroads. Handkerchief linen or lawn was another type of very thin, soft linen that was used more in clothing and handkerchiefs than in household linens, but it is not unusual now to find fine doilies made of the fabric. Some types of needlework like Hardanger embroidery required special fabric that was made just for this work. Whether or not it had another name is unknown. It was always referred to simply as Hardanger cloth.

In the early days Indian Head, a heavy cotton fabric much like butcher's linen, was probably used more for clothing than for household linens. But from the forties onward when the war brides were trying to make linens for their new homes Indian Head became quite a favorite. It came in both white and colors. Lawn derived its name from Laon, France, where it was first made. It was also sometimes called India linon. First made of linen, it was later made of cotton. It was a soft fabric and was used sometimes for making dainty bridge cloths, napkins, and doilies. Linen cambric, a white linen fabric, was highly recommended for all types of church embroidery as well as all household linens. Marseilles, a heavy, double-faced white cotton fabric, was originally made in Marseilles, France. Used earlier for men's vest and maybe a few women's suits, it was finally used entirely for bedspreads with Bates Manufacturing Company leading the way.

One of the reasons it is so difficult today to distinguish one fabric from another in old linens is the fact that so many were almost identical, but were sold under different names. An example of this is one called Persian lawn. It was described as "similar to India linon only thinner and finer, yet stiffer and firmer than batiste, but not as sheer as organdy." If it was that similar when bought, say fifty years ago, think how it looks today after numerous washings. Pongee was a fabric woven from the cocoons of wild silkworms which feed on oak leaves and produced a coarser silk than that made from cultivated and mulberry-fed silkworms. Later a pongee, usually called a cotton pongee, would be made using cotton or mixing cotton and silk. This later fabric might be pongee-colored which was a light tan, or it could be dyed any color. It was used more for clothing, especially children's clothing, than for household linens although it was used quite a bit in art needlework. Ladies who made their curtains, and there were many who did, might use one of the so-called Swiss fabrics. One was known as curtain swiss. And then there was ticking. It was the one fabric that everybody knew and used. It began being made shortly after the mills were built, and it was bought and used by every housewife in America. In the beginning they had woven a linsey-woolsey type fabric to hold the leaves and corn husks they used to make mattresses. As the geese and other fowls began to multiply so did the feather beds, and for those they needed ticking—something woven tightly enough to hold the feathers.

Chapter Three
Pictures, Samplers, and Mottos

The first American sampler is believed to have been made by Loara Standish, daughter of Miles Standish and his second wife, Barbara. Other young girls who came to America either brought samplers they were working on or started new ones soon after their arrival. It was just something all young girls did. They had been made for a while before the settling of America, but like all ordinary things no records were kept, but it is known they were made long before that time and for a couple of centuries afterward. The reason they were so popular was the fact that samplers combined at least three very necessary skills—learning the alphabet, numbers, and sewing. Learning to do their stitches was probably the most important, but when they could combine the three it was certainly worthwhile. In fact, learning to make samplers became so important schools were opened just to teach the girls how to make them correctly. It was essential they go to the schools, especially if their mothers were not very skilled in needlework. These schools were usually run by unmarried or widowed ladies who were not only skilled in needlework, but also needed the money. Some even did the teaching as a sideline while working at other jobs. It was said that stage actresses who were experts with a needle often opened schools when they were not touring with a play.

In recent years the price of old samplers rose to such heights only the most affluent could afford them. And like everything in antiquedom, when the price rises so high reproductions surface. Apparently that has happened in the sampler field. Several years ago I met a lady at an antiques show who was displaying a couple of beautiful samplers. Maybe it was the price, maybe something else, I'm not sure but I got the feeling something was not exactly right. I asked her about them but she was hesitant to even discuss them. Her attitude seemed to be that there they are, if you want to buy them all right, if not someone else will. There was something about them that worried me so I kept talking to the other antique dealers in the show. Finally I found one who seemed to not only know the story but who would share it. She said the samplers were being made in The Maritimes (Canada). Seems some very skilled needleworker had been able to acquire fabric exactly like that used in the old samplers. She was then able to duplicate the old ones. We both agreed that no matter what she used or how she used it, they would still require some aging—unless of course she aged the fabric and the thread before she made the sampler. This dealer questioned whether the maker was doing the aging, or just selling them to dealers who did. If she was able to duplicate them, then there are others equally as skilled. But whether or not others have been made is unknown

as I have not seen any more that I actually questioned like those first two. But I am not an expert on samplers so maybe I could be deceived—easily.

It is easy to date samplers as most, if not all, have the date they were made embroidered on them, along with the name of the maker. There are a few stories about the girls later removing the dates from their samplers in order to lie about their ages. These samplers were kept hanging on the walls for years, which explains why the dates had to be removed—in fact, they were among the first things used to decorate the walls of the cabins or homes. Shortly thereafter there would be family portraits done by local artists, and then the embroidered pictures.

We tend to think of embroidered pictures as late bloomers, when actually they are about as old as samplers. Not nearly as many were made, it seems, but there is a record of them being made as early as the arrival of the Pilgrims. About the same time Loara Standish was making her sampler, Dame Brewster, wife of Elder Brewster, who played such an important part in settling Plymouth Plantation in Massachusetts, was working on an embroidered picture. The picture was of the English port of Plymouth, from which they had sailed only a few months earlier. She embroidered it while all the Pilgrims were still living aboard the Mayflower waiting for homes or shelters to be built in the New World. She could have been homesick and this was a permanent way of remembering her old home.

That was only the beginning. By the mid-1800s women were embroidering pictures of flowers, scenic views, their homes, and their dogs and cats. Not all of them were embroidered; some were crocheted while a few were tatted or knitted. Then there are the pictures some of the crocheters did of both wild or domestic animals. These pieces were framed and hung right along with all the other pictures, samplers, and mottos. When the walls became too cluttered with pictures, the older or less desirable ones were taken down, and the picture might be made into a pillow top. Decorative pillows were very popular then and still are, but no longer are many decorated with needlework as they once were. Some of the older pictures found today will show evidence of once having been used as a pillow top while some pillow tops will show they served a different purpose in another life. That trend continues today as we make pictures out of beautiful pillow tops, or pillow tops out of pictures. Perhaps that is the most fascinating thing about the old linens we collect—we can use them any way we want to, we can modernize our collection to fit our present needs.

Needlework mottos are another antique we tend to think of as quite modern. It isn't. Fifty years ago nearly every home in the country, especially in the rural areas, had at least one needlework motto. Our ancestors were a very religious people, after all they had come to America for religious freedom. They were thankful for both their homes and their freedom so for that reason they made pictures, actually mottos usually surrounded by a floral design. They ranged from "Home Sweet Home" to what almost amounted to a prayer of thanksgiving. The work might be embroidery, embellished in bright colors, needlepoint, or work on perforated paper. Later they would make small one-word mottos like Welcome or Merry Christmas to be framed and hung on the front door for special occasions.

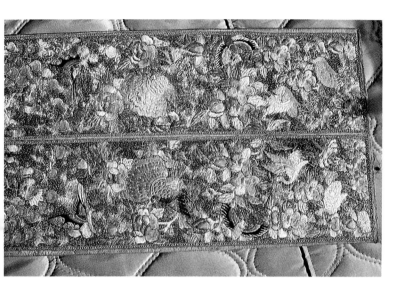

Chinese embroidery. $250-$300.

Early sampler sold at local auction recently for $1,300.

Sampler with 1822 date. $1,000-$1,300.

Home Sweet Home was a favorite topic for early needleworkers. $100-$125.

Tapestries like this have doubled and tripled in price in the past couple of decades. $125-$150.

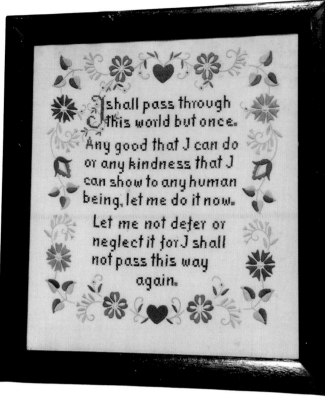

I shall pass through this world but once. Any good that I can do or any kindness that I can show to any human being, let me do it now. Let me not defer or neglect it for I shall not pass this way again.

Embroidering mottos like this one were popular in the fifties. $50-$75.

Late sampler of Martha's Vineyard, stamped and ready for embroidery. $8-$10.

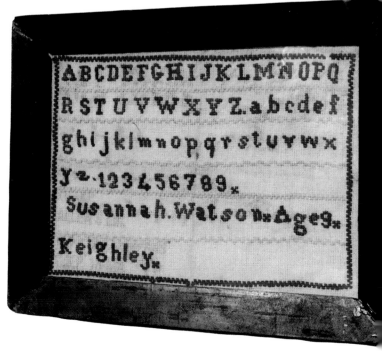

Late, undated sampler. $150-$200.

Fifties motto done in cross stitch. $45-$60.

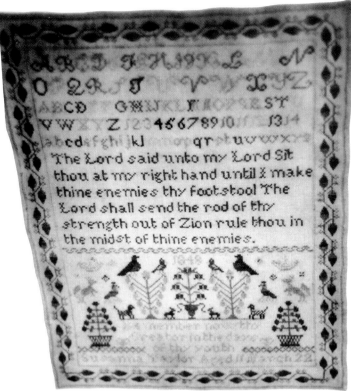

Early sampler. $900-$1,200.

Sampler with two dates, 1785 and 1799. $1,200-$1,500.

1838 sampler made by Harriet A. Squires. $900-$1,100.

In the thirties and forties making needlework Christmas decorations for the home was very popular. $25-$30.

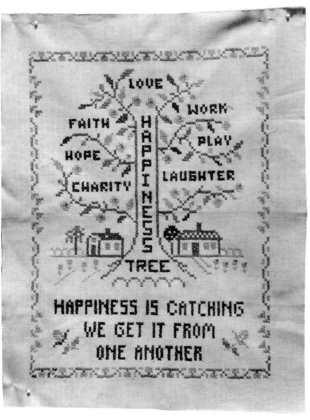

It is not too unusual to find pieces like this where the embroidery was never finished. For that reason it was not framed. $10-$15.

In the 1800s embroidery on perforated paper was very popular. $100-$150.

Eagle and *E Pluribus Unum* on blue banner. All done in cross stitch. $55-$75.

Many filet crochet pieces, like this one, were never framed. They could have been used for another purpose at some period. $17-$23.

This one could have also been made for a picture or a pillow top. $23-$28.

one was definitely made to be framed. $35-$40.

This filet crochet might have been made for a picture or a pillow top. $25-$30.

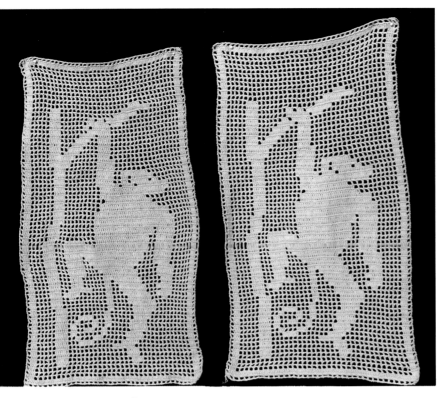

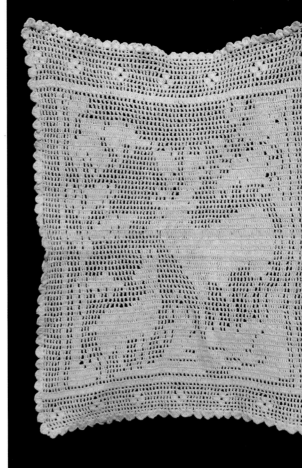

Pair of filet crochet monkeys made in two colors. Could have been made to be used in child's room. $25-$35 pair.

There can be little doubt this piece was also made to be framed. $30-$40.

Could have been a wall hanging—or an unframed picture. $20-$24.

Although the cow was a familiar animal, it is uncertain how the maker intended to use this one. $15-$20.

Embroidered and needlepoint pictures
with ribbons they won at the Tennessee State Fair in the fifties and sixties.

Framed picture of embroidered
flowers. $50-$75.

Embroidered picture frame, the type
women like to make as gifts for men.
$40-$50.

Filet crochet of a pair of camels. $25-$35.

Another needlepainting by Reet Pukk done in 1962. The poem "Birchtrees" is written on the back in both Esthonian and English. $100-$135.

Picture embroidered in silk thread with the following written on the back: *"Winter in the Mountains" Needlepainting by Reet Pukk, Esthonian artist, age 67, 1962.* $85-$115.

Beautifully embroidered butterflies with flowers. $10-$15.

Picture of elderly Oriental man, made entirely of scraps of silk fabric. $25-$40.

Floral design embroidered on black. $20-$25.

Embroidered picture frame with child's photo. $25-$35.

of flowers done in needlepoint. $35-$45.

Unusual picture due to the fact the cross and flowers are done in petit point and needlepoint while the background (canvas) is left plain. Note on back indicates it was framed in Greece. $75-$100.

Embroidered picture. $20-$25.

Embroidering small pictures of flowers and vegetables to hang in the kitchen was popular in the sixties. $15-$20 for three.

Embroidered picture of swan and flowers. $20-$25.

Small embroidered flowers. $12-$15 for two.

Needlepoint picture of dog and bird. $50-$75.

Embroidered picture that sold at a local auction last year for $450.

Colorful needlepoint picture with notation across the bottom "A present from India in 1889." $75-$100 unframed.

Another style of embroidered kitchen pictures. $15-$20 for three.

Reverse of Oriental embroidery showing how beautifully it was done.

Another embroidered picture obviously part of a pair. $50-$75.

Oriental embroidery, silk thread on silk fabric. Very intricate. $50-$75.

Chapter Four
Pillow Cases

A century ago, one of the favorite sayings of needleworkers was "Anything given to the mother is given to the whole family." This probably made them feel noble when they showered a friend or family member with household linens they had made. It wasn't nearly as big a sacrifice for them as it would be for the average woman today, who is doing a dozen things at one time, whereas the biggest chore most of our ancestors had by that time was doing more needlework. Of course there were still the farm families and the ones moving westward, but generally those living in the cities and town were having a much easier time than they had ever known.

By the turn of the present century most men were making the living for the family without help from their wives. Finally, she was free to do what she wanted. In many cases that was doing more needlework. By this time even the average family had a maid or two which left the wife with more free time to work on any of the arts and crafts she enjoyed. Thousands of them must have settled on needlework, if we are to judge by the large amount still available today. By working steadily all day every day, even if she worked very slowly, she could not avoid accumulating more household linens than she would ever be able to use. So, she, like all the other needleworkers, decided to give some of her pieces away as gifts. This solution didn't exactly solve her storage problem because while the homemaker was sharing her pieces with others, she was also being reciprocated by receiving pieces of needlework others had made. Everybody was sharing their work whether it was needlework, china painting, basketry, or pyrography. This seems to have been one of the biggest gift giving periods in this country with pillow cases, scarves, and towels leading the way.

The pillow case or pillow slip as it was originally called is one of the few things no homemaker today could probably live without. When researching their history, it turns out that they just seem to have evolved—out of necessity and the need for beauty. The majority of the early settlers in America made mattresses using leaves, then they worked up to corn husks as soon as they learned to grow corn. The next step was the feather bed, and there can be little doubt that when Americans discovered the luxury of the feather mattress they just had to make some feather pillows. In the beginning the settlers are believed to have used mattress covers they had woven themselves, probably linsey-woolsey. But as soon as ticking became available, it was used almost exclusively. It was and still is the best as it was the only fabric that was woven so tightly the feathers could not escape. For a while some people might sleep on the ticking pillows without benefit of a case or slip, but as soon

as they were settled and could afford it, they made pillow cases. The early housewives might have used plain cases for everyday use, but for show and tell they made and used some of the most elaborate pillow cases they were able to make.

We have to remember that those early housewives had little leisure time and even less money to buy a few necessities, much less luxuries. In those early days pillow cases would have been sheer luxury. But as the farm became cleared and chores became a little lighter, the housewives began to think about a little beauty for their otherwise drab homes and soon found their needlework would brighten every corner. They made curtains for the windows, cloths for the tables, and bedspreads and pillow cases for the beds. As time passed it became easier and easier to acquire fabric for pillow cases, in fact about a century ago they had a choice of sheeting or muslin to make cases. Believe it or not about that time many were made of linen—with matching linen sheets. Pillow tubing became available about that time as did printed fabric with a colored border so the maker could simply cut her pillow cases and seam them up on the sewing machine. Since these were figured they were never embroidered, but many sets have been seen with crocheted, knitted, or tatted lace using the same colors as those in the fabric. By the twenties one could obtain pillow cases, stamped for embroidery, by simply selling two or three subscriptions to various magazines. *Needlecraft Magazine* seems to have been the leader in this field. Nearly every monthly issue through the twenties, thirties, and forties offered a choice of one or more pairs of stamped cases free to the person or persons selling two or three annual subscriptions to the publication. Money might not have been too plentiful, but it shouldn't have been that difficult to sell a subscription at only 50 cents each. In the thirties, *Needlecraft* began offering stamped pillow cases for sale. In August 1938 they offered a full page ad of pillow cases at reduced prices. Ten different designs stamped on 42 inch white tubing was offered for 98 cents to $1.10 each. Floss to embroider the cases was offered at prices ranging from 28 cents to 44 cents per case. On cases where crocheted cotton was required to make the edging, the cost usually ran about 15 cents.

In their 1927 catalog of Art Needlework and Fancy Wear for Women and Children, Frederick Herrschner, Inc., Chicago, offered two pairs of pillow cases "stamped on good quality linen-finish tubing and hemstitched for crochet edging" for $1.29 each. Included in that price was enough Nun's "boilproof" cotton to do the embroidery. This new embroidery thread was described as "an imported cotton of highest quality and guaranteed Boilproof and Sunfast in all shades." Since this was a time when coordinating bedroom linens was important, dresser scarves matching the pillow cases were also offered for 89 cents each. In the same catalog they offered two appliquéd pillow cases, one with pink hearts hemstitched on and the other with "Prim little hemstitched baskets of blue." They were rather expensive at $1.95, and the embroidery thread was extra at 25 cents for enough to do a pair.

Colorful pillow cases that came absolutely free were made from feed and grain sacks in the thirties, forties, and fifties. The manufacturers of the feed and grain bought by the farmers probably latched onto the idea of using printed sacks or bags in order to sell more than his competitor. It worked. Farmers, dairymen, and people raising chickens for the market refused to buy feed that wasn't in printed bags. As soon as the feed was used the housewife washed and starched those bags to make clothing for the children and linens for the home. If they

had a large operation, they divided the extra bags with friends and neighbors. Pillow cases made from those bags can sometimes be found today. They are still quite pretty, especially when the maker edged them in crochet lace using the colors in the bag.

Another reason for the plentiful supply of pillow cases today could be they were so highly touted as *the* necessary item for one's hope chest. An example is an article in a 1924 issue of *Modern Priscilla*. It began with "No hope chest or linen closet is complete without its quota of hand-decorated pillow slips, and there is such a variety of ways to embellish these essential linens that it is sometimes hard to choose." But choose they did, and we can see the results of that choice today when we see stacks of pillow slips displayed at antiques shows by linen dealers.

One of a pair of pillow cases made of floral feed or grain bags, crocheted lace edging. $15-$20 pair.

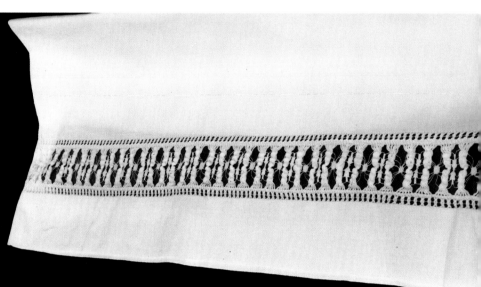

Victorians used ribbon on everything including lacing it through the drawn work on these pillow cases. $30-$35 pair.

Same pillow cases without the ribbon. Same price.

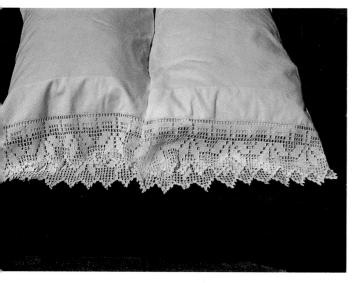

Pair of pillow cases with 6 inch wide crocheted lace. $30-$40 pair.

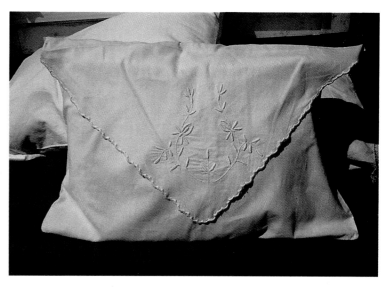

Envelope-type pillow case, often made as singles. $12-$15 each.

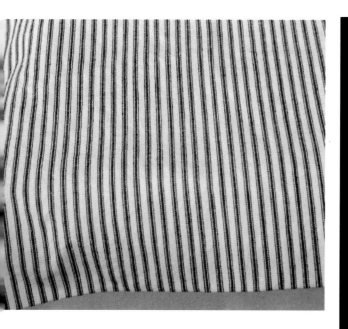

Before the pillow cases were needed the homemaker had to make the pillows. The most popular were made of blue and white ticking, as it was woven tightly enough to hold the feathers

Pillow cases with floral embroidery and crocheted edging. $20-$28 pair.

An example of the machine embroidered pillow cases that were sold in the forties and fifties, beautifully boxed, to be given as gifts, generally Christmas gifts. The thinly woven fabric was so full of starch and filler they looked like fine percale. But one washing later only a limp rag was left. One woman described them at the time as being "so thin straws could be shot through them." When found starched and ironed today, they look fair to middling. $5-$9.

Pair of pillow cases stamped but never embroidered. They are only valuable to someone who would like to complete them, or who would like to have them for the rarity. $15-$22.

Same unworked pillow cases showing the name of the maker, copyright date (1921), and original price tag.

Same unworked pillow cases showing the colored pieces stamped for appliqué.

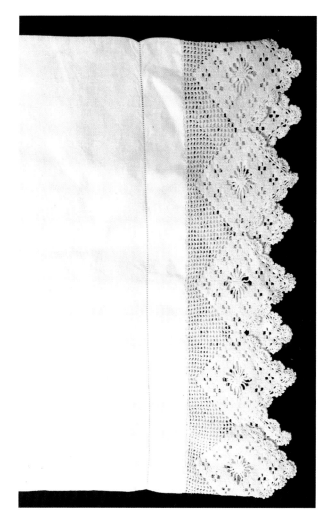

Pillow case with wide crocheted lace. $25-$35 pair.

Early needleworkers could obtain pillow cases in several ways. They could even make their own from scratch and then stamp the design they wanted on them, or they could get them free just by selling a couple of subscriptions to magazines like *Needlecraft*. Old copies of the magazine, which are filled with needlework ideas, can now be found for prices ranging from $3 to $7 each.

Pillow cases from the forties and fifties, basket design, scalloped edge. $16-$20 pair.

Pillow cases with 6 inch wide crocheted lace. $30-$40 pair.

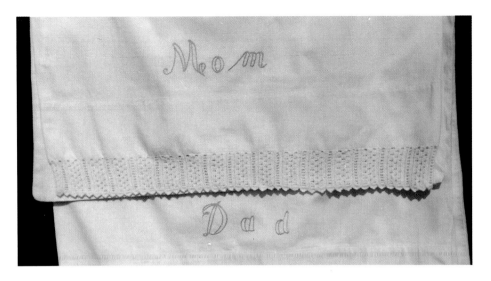

Crocheted lace is poor quality, embroidery even poorer.
Inexperienced needleworker probably made this set as a gift
for parents. $10-$15 pair.

These pillow cases appear to have been made of feed or
grain bags. The edging which is rick rack and crochet was
very popular in the fifties. $17-$25 pair.

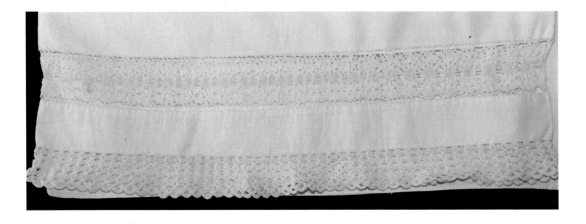

Pillow cases with crocheted edging and insertion. $30-$40
pair.

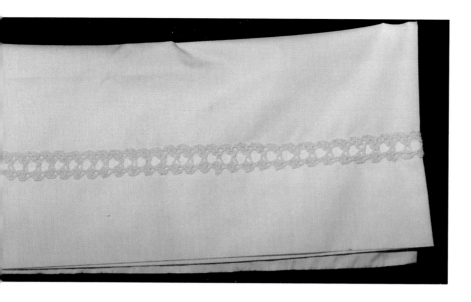

Crochet covers the seam on the top of the deep hem on this pair. $18-$23 pair.

Pillow cases with monogram and crocheted lace. $23-$28 pair.

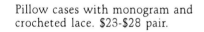

One of a pair of linen pillow cases that came with matching linen sheets, Name *Purdy* embroidered on both sheet and pillow cases. Wide knitted lace. $35-$50 pair.

Pillow cases made of factory-printed pillow fabric that could be bought by the yard. A homemaker only had to cut the fabric to fit her pillows and seam it up. $12-$16 pair.

Pair of hand embroidered pillow cases still in the gift box they have been in since the fifties. $19-$25 pair.

Blue and white figured feed or grain sacks were used to make these pillow cases, trimmed with blue and white crochet. $17-$22 pair.

Pair of embroidered pillow cases. $18-$24 pair.

Short, single pillow case with the letter B in filet crochet, probably for a child's bed. Crocheted lace. $10-$15 each.

Embroidered white-on-white pillow cases with narrow crocheted lace. $19-$26 pair.

Embroidered swans on lake, pink crocheted lace. $20-$28 pair.

Pillow cases were premium for selling subscriptions to *Needlecraft Magazine*. Cross stitch. $19-$27 pair.

Crocheted lace on plain pillow cases. $18-$25 pair.

Plain pillow cases, wide hem, crocheted lace with points. $18-$24 pair.

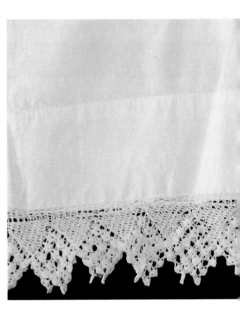

Pillow cases with plain but wide crocheted lace. $27-$33 pair.

Fringed and crocheted lace, unusual on pillow cases. $22-$30 pair.

Embroidered sunbonnet girl with umbrella, narrow crocheted lace. $18-$27 pair.

Another pair of pillow cases with wide crocheted lace. $25-$30 pair.

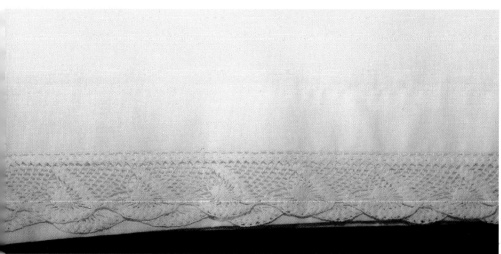

Pillow cases with medium width crocheted lace. $22-$27 pair.

Pillow cases with knitted lace. $25-$30 pair.

Pillow case with wide knitted lace. $23-$27 pair.

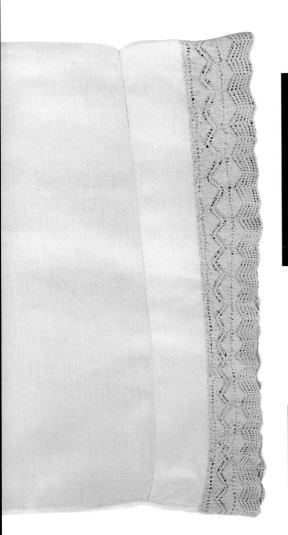

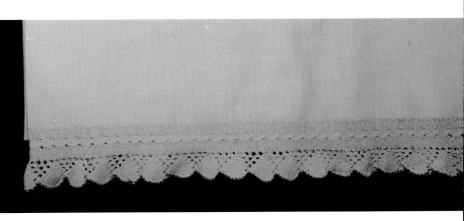

Knowing how much work had gone into the making of the lace on pillow cases, the owners often took lace off worn cases, and put it on new ones. That was the case with these later colored ones. $17-$22 pair.

Letter H in filet crochet is only decoration on these pillow cases. $16-$20 pair.

The knitted lace on these pillow cases is very similar to that used on the ones above. $25-$30 pair.

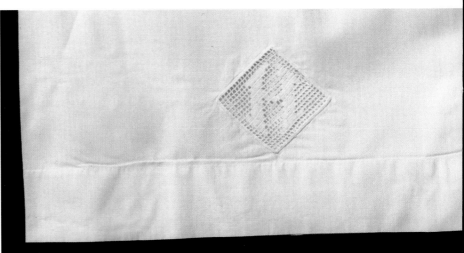

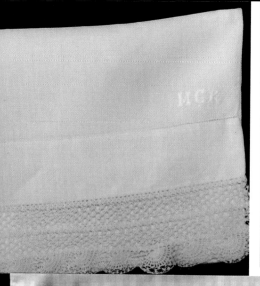
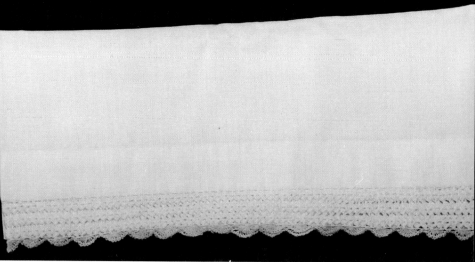

Yellow border on white crocheted lace dates it after 1950. $19-$23 pair.

Yellow checked, gingham pillow cases decorated along the hem with a cross design usually found in drawn work. $16-$24 pair.

Appliquéd flowers and leaves decorate these pillow cases. $18-$23 pair.

Printed pillow case fabric like this could be bought by the yard. $3-$5 yard.

Fancy monogrammed pillow cases with scalloped border. $18-$25 pair.

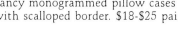

Chapter Five
Pillow Shams and Bolsters

One interesting aspect of antiquing is watching how various items grow in popularity. Twenty-five years ago it was almost unheard of to find household linens offered in a show, and actually, they weren't that plentiful in shops. Within the last decade the number of collectors has grown to such proportions it was not surprising recently to see an ad for an all-textile show. Admittedly it wasn't all household linens, there was some clothing, but imagine a show consisting of all textiles. Nearly all antiques shows today have one or more textile dealers who specialize or deal exclusively in fabrics while many of the show dealers will have several pieces, maybe a small display. Whereas reports of upcoming shows once stressed the number of furniture or glass exhibitors with descriptions of their finer pieces, the trend has changed. Now there is mention of the textile dealers with information on what they will be offering.

Even more interesting is the amount available. We tend to think of fabric as "soft goods," the term actually used by many stores in the forties. For some unknown reason some of us tend to think the hand loomed fabric was stronger or tougher than the factory-made, and pieces like linsey-woolsey sheets, blankets, and coverlets can still be found. Most are a hundred years old or older. But we also find factory-made pieces that have stood the test of time. The latter is much more plentiful, and that can be attributed to the fact more of it was made. All of these fabrics are probably much tougher than first was thought because some of these pieces have suffered much use and abuse through the years. We are so careful today in where and how we use our linens, yet our ancestors used these same pieces daily and usually washed them weekly. This could go on for half a century. Of course they continued to make new linens all the time to replace the ones that wore out. They were careful when they ironed their linens, not so much to save them as to make them look pretty when used. When they had finished ironing a piece, especially embroidered pieces, they ironed it once more on the wrong or underside. This made the embroidery stand out so that it was more attractive.

This didn't apply as much to pillow shams and bolsters as to some of the other linens, probably because not as many people used them, nor were they used on a regular basis. Although they were used regularly in some homes, there were others where they were only used on Sunday or when guests were expected. Bolsters are believed to have been more popular than shams because so many bed spreads were made with a separate bolster. In some case the extra bolster was made in addition to the one attached to the bedspread. This is especially true of the homemade bedspreads. Separate bolsters have been seen with homemade chenille spreads as well as the knotted ones made in the Great Smokey and Blue Ridge Mountains. Only two or three extra bolsters have been seen with embroidered bedspreads, and this was probably just a case of wanting to make the extra piece in an effort to change the appearance of the bed. Extra bolsters were made with many of the factory-made bedspreads, especially those made at Bates Mills, Lewiston, Maine.

Now shams are another story altogether. To use the shams to an advantage you had to have the right kind of bed which was the solid headboard wooden bed, either the old walnut or the later oak. The big, fluffy feather pillows could be propped against those headboards to show off the shams to an advantage. All the shams we have seen were handmade. One pair that is different is shown in the illustrations. They were crocheted and made to fit over the pillow like a case. It had to be a sham as it would have been very uncomfortable sleeping on a crocheted case. Most shams are embroidered so that was probably just a case where the maker wanted crocheted shams and didn't know how to make them stay on the pillow except as a case.

Some of the shams were monogrammed while others had things like "Joyful Awakening" on them. All were made in pairs, some with identical wording on the shams while others had different wordings on each, such as the example with the lady sleeping as fairies danced overhead. It says, "I slept and dreamed that life was beauty." The other shows her sweeping and says, "I awoke and found that life was duty." Some of the shams have fabric ruffles around the outside; others have lace, in some cases factory-made lace.

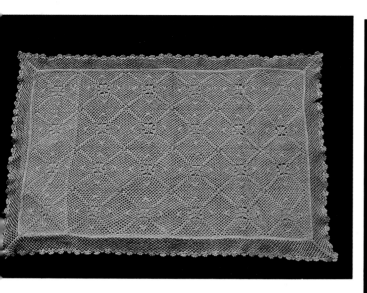

Probably made originally as a crocheted pillow sham with the back being added later to hold it in place. $30-$38 pair.

Handmade chenille bolster that goes with a matching bedspread. Made in the fifties for a child's bed. Not very useful nor very desirable without the spread.

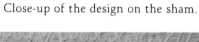

Close-up of the design on the sham.

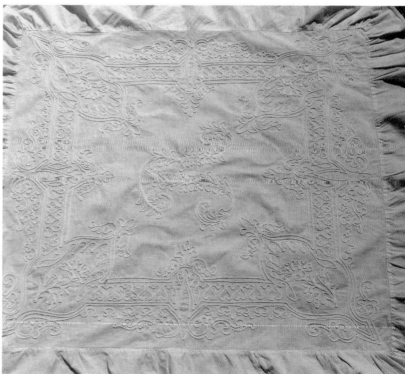

Heavily embroidered, white-on-white shams. $40-$45 pair.

This is not one of the regulation bolsters that was tucked around the pillows; instead it is a bed width pillow case open at both ends to hold two pillows in bolster shape. Monogrammed, made in singles since only one was needed. $25-$30 each.

Close-up of embroidery in center of bolster or pillow case.

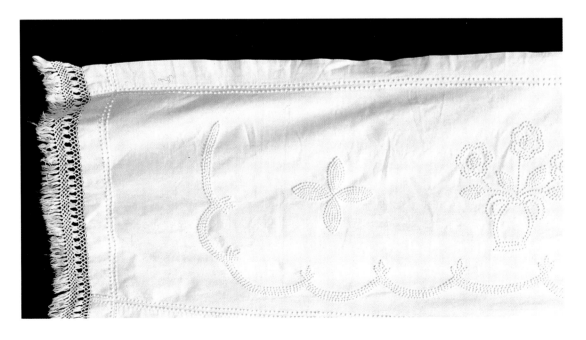

Knotted bolster made to be used with Knotted bedspread. Fringe also handmade. $40-$75.

Factory-made bolster to be used with matching bedspread. Of little use without the bedspread.

White-on-white, heavily embroidered sham. $40-$50 pair.

Close-up of embroidery.

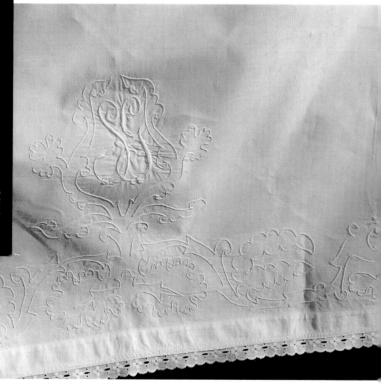

Monogrammed, linen pillow sham, one of a pair. Wide lace all around. $35-$45 pair.

One of a pair of shams embroidered in turkey red. $25-$35 pair.

Sham with floral embroidery done in turkey red. $35-$45 pair.

One of a pair of shams done in turkey red. One has Good Night while the other has Good Morning embroidered on it. $45-$55 pair.

Go to Sleep With the Flowers is embroidered in turkey red on this sham. $36-$45 pair.

40

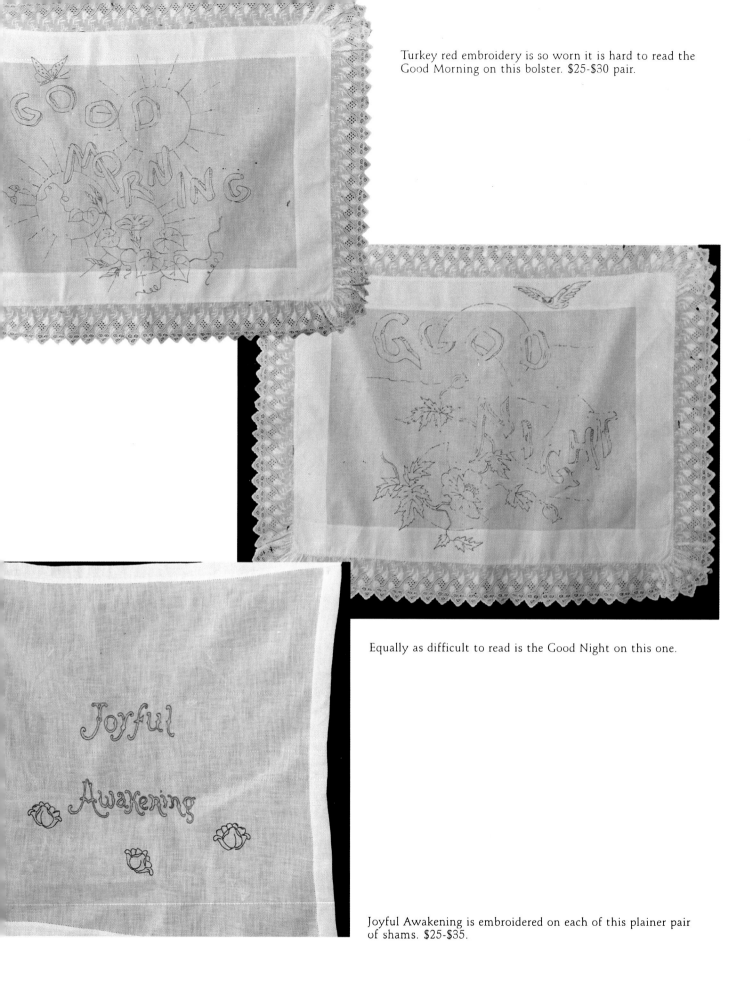

Turkey red embroidery is so worn it is hard to read the Good Morning on this bolster. $25-$30 pair.

Equally as difficult to read is the Good Night on this one.

Joyful Awakening is embroidered on each of this plainer pair of shams. $25-$35.

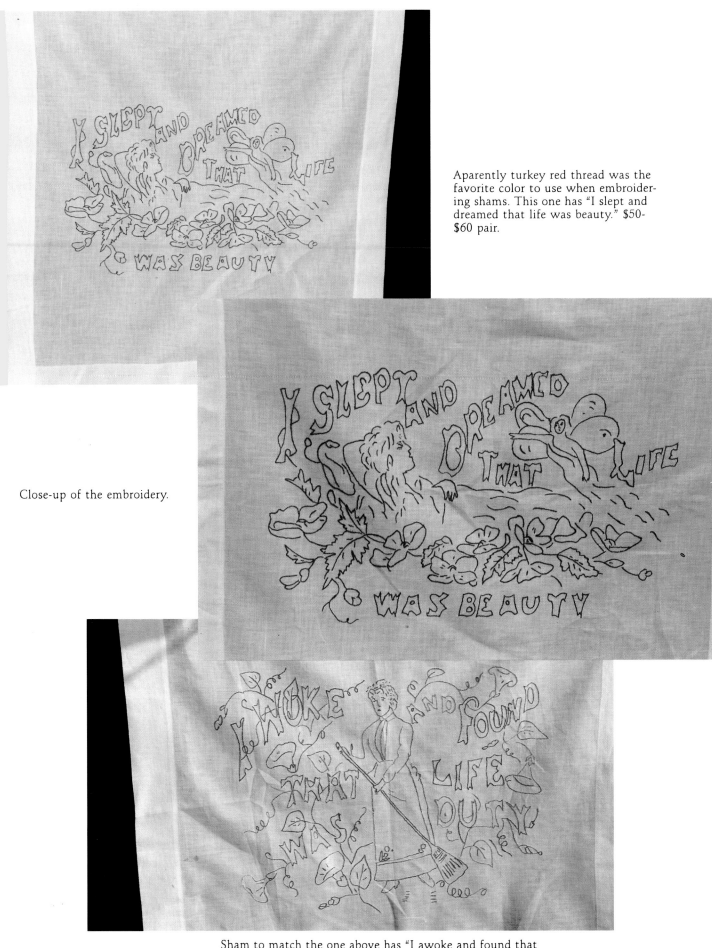

Aparently turkey red thread was the favorite color to use when embroidering shams. This one has "I slept and dreamed that life was beauty." $50-$60 pair.

Close-up of the embroidery.

Sham to match the one above has "I awoke and found that life was duty."

Chapter Six
Quilts and Coverlets

Sixty-five years ago an editor at *Needlecraft Magazine* wrote an editorial on the merits of needlework. At that time needlework was considered a form of art, in fact, many described embroidery as needle painting. They felt that the pictures they made with their needles was as worthy of praise as those done with paint and a brush.

The subtitle of the *Needlecraft* article was *Encourage Needle-Art in the Children*, and it began "In this day and age of machinery, the most worthy things to cultivate and cherish is art. Why does grandmother's sampler merit the choice wall space among our masterpieces of renown? Not alone for its simple beauty nor for the reason that it was fashioned by beloved hands, but because machinery cannot duplicate it. It has individuality. And why should dear old Aunt Mary's patchwork quilt be so coveted by the wealthy Mrs. Van Pelt? Because the tiny stitches, those brilliant patches of gingham cannot be found in stores—not for all the dollars she offers."

Things have changed some since that was written because new quilts can now be bought in the stores, but they don't have the tiny stitches mentioned in the editorial nor are they made with the old fabrics. Admittedly quilts continue to be made today, one tiny stitch after another, each sewn with the love and patience used on the old ones, but these are much more expensive than those found offered for sale in the stores and in catalogs. The majority of those offered for sale in those sources are handmade, its true, but in most cases they were made in China. Then there is a very cheap version of quilts that is made of fabric printed to resemble the old quilts and they are machine stitched, not hand stitched.

Although needlework was frequently given as gifts by the makers during the heyday of the so-called craft revival, nevertheless it was usually given to a person the maker thought would treasure it. Then there were instances when it had to be given to a person who had given the maker some of her work. They might not have really wanted to give it and could have felt the recipient's work was not worthy of exchange, but custom decreed they must. Part of this can be attributed to editorials like the one quoted above from *Needlecraft* that continued with "Things that are created with the human hand, those rare pieces of workmanship, are of great value, nearly priceless. They require skill, patience and the touch that only an artist can impart." The writer was talking about the exquisite pieces, where the embroidery done was correctly, the tatting, crochet, and knitting that was done to perfection as well as the quilts that were pieced in beautiful patterns. Those were the pieces that were treasured then and are still treasured today. Pieces were made then for "everyday use" just as they are today, but the really elegant pieces, the ones on which they lavished so much love and work, are the ones that will bring the big prices today.

My family like all the others in our area made two types of quilts. For everyday use the quilts were pieced from scraps of old clothing, undamaged panels from dresses that might be too worn to wear even around the house, tails of shirts that hadn't faded due to the fact they were worn inside the trousers and not exposed to the sun, outgrown children's clothes when there was no longer any smaller children to pass them down to, and even scraps from discarded aprons. There would be little pressure on the fabric once it was quilted as it was only used for warmth. That meant the fabric didn't have to be new to use in everyday quilts, but it helped if the colors were bright—but actually there weren't too many fabrics in those days that would be considered real bright. Calico and gingham were the favorite fabrics for dresses that would be worn around the house and to school. Much of the fabric was in black and white figured, very dull, but didn't show soil. The gingham was a little brighter, however. It came in blues and greens, the favorites. Lavenders and yellows were less popular for two reasons—they were a little more expensive and they showed soil more easily, according to some mothers. Regardless of the problems a family with two or three children might have, the mother managed somehow to make a new quilt or two every year. This kept a good supply on hand all the time. One of the interesting things about quilting in our area was the fact that after church a parishioner would share the news that she was "putting up" a quilt next week. The other ladies would inquire about the day she would have it ready to quilt, and all would plan to help her "get it out." In those days all the women could sympathize with one another about getting a quilt out. The maker could piece the quilt alone, she could even fasten the top, lining and cotton onto the quilting frames, but from there on she needed help. Not because she didn't enjoy the actual quilting, but because one entire room of the house was needed for the quilt until it was finished. When the quilt was first put on the frame it had to be extended to the size of the quilt and that meant it either had to be hung from the ceiling or straight chairs placed under each corner. Then there had to be enough space for the quilters to get around the frame. As the quilting was completed on either side, the frames with the quilt attached were rolled over which helped by giving more space. But the quilt had to be completed before the furniture could be brought back and the room restored to its original use.

Not all quilts were made out of worn clothing, as the ladies also saved scraps from leftover dressmaking. They might even buy a few yards of new fabric just to make a fancy quilt, or to supplement scraps left over from making school clothes. Around the thirties a new quilt fad swept the country; the so-called Yo-Yo Quilt. The edge or hem of a circle of fabric was gathered to form a smaller circle. These circles were tacked together on the sides to form a quilt. Matching pillows were also made. But the most outstanding quilts were the ones called Crazy Quilts. They were made of scraps of luxury fabric like satins and velvets. But the Victorians made them even more beautiful by covering each seam with spidery embroidery and then embroidering fantastic flowers and birds on the various pieces. You can't call them squares because they were whatever shape they were in when put together, hence the name Crazy Quilt.

Two types of coverlets are available today, neither in plentiful supply. The first is the native-made. It was made by anyone with a home loom, but appears to have been most popular in the mountains of Tennessee, Kentucky, North Carolina, and Virginia. The weather didn't get cold enough to require heavy wool coverlets in the deep south and in the north as well as the border states they had the itinerant weavers who roamed the country with their Jacquard looms. These coverlets are easily distinguishable from the mountain-made coverlets because of their elaborate, naturalistic designs or patterns. Birds, flowers, emblems, houses, and scrolls were the usual designs while the native loom-made coverlets had a much plainer design. It was said that the Jacquard weavers had been trained in Europe where textile weaving was more highly developed than in the rural areas of this country. And the mechanical equipment of their looms allowed them to do work that was impossible on local looms. Like other trades of that era, the Jacquard loom men soon established routes with regular customers that they visited year after year. The housewife would have her yarn ready and they would weave it into a new coverlet. It is easy to distinguish these coverlets from the ones called "kiverlids" made by the mountain makers. The Jacquard had a more elaborate design while the ones made in the mountains and elsewhere were made in two pieces and sewn together. Since the looms would only weave pieces about three feet wide it was necessary to weave two matching pieces and sew them together. Some of the pieces are so well matched and sewn so carefully it is almost impossible to find the seam. Then there are some that are not as well matched nor sewn as well, but if you find one that doesn't have a seam at all, not even on close examination, you can rest assured it is factory-made, not made on a home loom. Both the Jacquard and the home loomed coverlet will be quite expensive when found today.

Quilts have gained favor in recent years as table coverings. $250-$300.

Over 200 small pieces were required to make this appliquéd quilt. Circa 1950 stamped design from Bucilla. $400-$500.

Lovely appliquéd quilt. $500-$600.

Dealer offering this quilt at a show knew neither the history nor the pattern. $400.

Quilt made of less colorful fabric. $350-$400.

Good colors and quilting. $400-$500.

Quilt originally pre-stamped for appliqué and embroidery.
Seersucker fabric, circa 1950. $150-$200.

Late blue and white quilt, excellent
workmanship. $375-$500.

Crazy quilt made of silk and satin scraps, then embroidered.
$275-$400.

Another late quilt, very colorful, excellent workmanship.
$400-$500.

46

This quilt sold at a local auction for $450.

Quilt displayed at an antiques show. Priced $550.

Red and white quilt displayed on an Adirondack bench. $300-$350.

Crazy quilt first made in squares, then put together and embroidered. $300-$400.

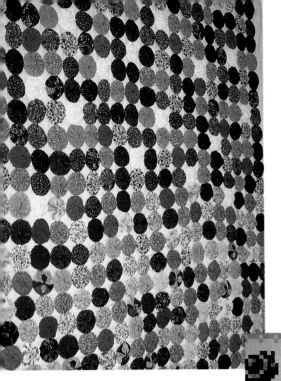

Yo-Yo quilts were made of small, round, gathered circles that were later sewn together. They have no lining, nor are they quilted, hence not as desirable. $150-$200.

Late appliquéd quilt, excellent quilting. $400-$500.

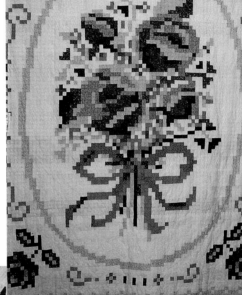

Colorful appliquéd quilt. $450-$600.

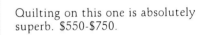

Quilting on this one is absolutely superb. $550-$750.

Center of a quilt that was done in cross stitch. Probably pre-stamped. $450-$550.

Earthtone colored fabrics were used to make this quilt in the Star of Texas design. $500-$600.

Fancy Yo-Yo quilt with solid color Yo-Yos forming a design in the center. $200-$250.

Chapter Seven
Rugs

Of all the handcrafted rugs made through the years (and there were many types), none reached the popularity of the hooked rugs. They are still very sought after and prices haven't peaked yet. Along with good furniture they seem to attract the most attention and the most competitive bidding at any estate auction.

Like so many of the crafts of that period, rugs were accepted as a necessity, not a luxury. It was not necessary to keep records or explain how they were made as the directions were passed from mother to daughter, or maybe friend to friend. Perhaps this sentence from the book *Homecraft Rugs*, published in 1929, best describes it: "The history of rug craft is one of storied interest, not written, but wrought in strands of yarn, silk, flax, hemp, and cotton." In recent years a few theories have been introduced, but unfortunately none can be reconciled with the other. There are those who believe the hooked rug originated with the Viking families who referred to hooking as "rhye," which meant "torn cloth." One group thought maybe it began with the Moors of southern Spain while another thought it might have originated with the Danes and Norsemen. Still another theory is that the rugs were first made in England and Scotland. There is a strong likelihood that the hooked rug as we know it today originated in the Maritime Provinces of Canada and quickly spread to New England and on into Pennsylvania. Many, many hooked rugs were made in these areas over a very long period of time and are still being made today. Hooked rugs are also known to have been made in the southern part of the country, especially the mountain regions, however few examples can be found there and even less that are known to have been made there.

Wills and inventories have always been a good source for determining how our ancestors felt about their worldly possessions. Everything they owned was listed, including in one will a spittoon that sold for 5 cents. Also in that 1873 listing of items sold at "public outcry" was one parlor carpet, more than likely an Oriental carpet that sold for $3 at the sale, and another listed simply as a rug that sold for 25 cents. There can be little doubt that last one was a handcrafted rug, probably a hooked, or just maybe a braided rug. One of the reasons for the failure to mention anything about the handcrafted rugs could have been the fact they were made from scraps, scraps left over from old clothing or from yarn left over from another project, therefore they were not considered valuable or worthy of mention. Another reason could have been the fact they were made primarily to cover wide board floors, or maybe even dirt floors, just to make them warmer. Since they were walked on constantly, they didn't last as long as other handmade pieces like the bedrugs or cupboard cloths. Incidentally, the cupboard cloths will be found in old wills listed as "cubberd cloths."

The first handmade rugs, those made specifically to be used as rugs and nothing else, are believed to have been made around 1775. These are also believed to have been the first made with beauty in mind, that is, with designs and coordinated colors. It seems that hooked rug makers really hit their stride around the time of the Civil War as several beautiful, dated examples have been seen. The earlier rugs were first made on a base of homespun linen, and later on tow and burlap. A type of burlap is still used on the few that are being made today.

Another group thinks that hooked rugs originated from "thrumming," a process of fastening short, cut-off pieces of yarn or cloth known as thrums to a background of fabric. A version of this type work is still used on a very limited basis in some areas today. The thrums were worked through the holes in very loosely woven fabric leaving the two ends on one side. Thrumming is not the same as hooking, but it is so closely associated one method could have originated from the other. The difference in the two is the fact that in hooking the uncut strips are pulled through the fabric with a hook to form loops that are not cut.

A person had to have lots of artistic ability to create a design for a realistic looking hooked rug. It seems more people lacked this talent than had it; therefore this demand for hooked rug designs made one man quite rich. That man was E. S. Frost, a Union soldier who returned to his Biddeford, Maine, home after the war. He had been injured and was left a semi-invalid. He still had to earn a living, and he needed to get outside for his health's sake so he became a peddler of tin utensils. In that capacity he traveled around the farms and villages of Maine, New Hampshire, and Rhode Island selling and mending tin items. Most of his customers not only wanted to buy new tin and have their old repaired, but in the course of his travels he found the women were almost begging for new hooked rug patterns and designs. In an effort to see if they were really serious about the new patterns and designs, he and his wife made up a few for him to take on his next trip. They sold so well and so fast he decided he should make some stencils so he could make numerous stamped rugs at one time. Mr. Frost was another of our ingenious ancestors who used what he had to make what he needed, or at least what he thought would work for him. Using old copper wash boilers (sometimes called ham boilers) he had bartered for on his rounds, he flattened them on an anvil, and then using chisels and files he made the design on them. He didn't make the stencils to sell, but rather to print the designs on burlap and then sell the stamped rug base. His sales increased and he continued to improve and create more designs. Finally he was printing them in color. This helped the less talented to make exquisite rugs in realistic colors. In time Mr. Frost became so successful he stopped his tin route and opened a shop that specialized in hooked rug patterns and designs. Reports are Mr. Frost made enough money in his rug design business to move to California. But again his health failed. No records could be found of what happened to him after that.

Seeing how lucrative the Frost business had become, others followed, and with his move to California it left the field wide open. By this time not only were professional designers furnishing patterns, there were numerous talented people designing their own—and maybe a few extras for sale. Not unlike other creative crafts many people did variations of well known designs creating even more designs. That helps to explain why there are still so many available hooked rugs now in so many patterns.

Rugs will be found with designs of things that were familiar to both the designer and the maker, things like flowers, birds, and animals, especially the family dog. Then there were pictures of houses, sometimes that of the owner, other times just any old house. Then as now cats were a favorite pet so it was natural for them to be used on rugs. Deer was another favorite, especially for those living in deer country. Farmyard fowls, especially ducks and geese, were used often. Apparently not too many rugs were made using a train design as those with that design can bring the bidders to their feet at any auction. Rug designers often copied portions of famous paintings or Currier and Ives prints. In most cases it helps to date the rug. Those copied after the Currier and Ives prints will usually date around the late 1800s while those with an automobile in the design has to have been made in the early 1900s.

Not all of the choice rugs were hooked, but they seem to be the pick of the litter because of the high prices they bring today. Next in line for choice is the braided or plaited rug. The origin of the braided rug like most needlecraft has been lost in the vale of antiquity. However it is believed to have originated in England and was then brought to the New World by the English who settled here. Chances are the first braided rugs were made using sedge grass and corn husks, not together, but each used to make its own rug. The cold New England winters demanded a warmer rug so when the colonists were able to acquire enough textiles they began using them in rug making, a lot of them of the braided variety. This trend continues today with many people still making the braided rugs according to the methods used by their mothers while others are creating their own methods. Through the years men have made a few rugs, but it is surprising today how many are braiding rugs both for relaxation—and for the money, as newly braided rugs are also selling for good prices. A little pamphlet titled *How to Braid a Rug in One Day* was published in 1949. They were either referring to a very small rug, or they planned for the braider to have all her materials ready to start putting together, and even then it would have to be a small rug, if it was going to made in one

day. The interesting thing about this booklet was the suggestions for using strips of rug braiding on other things like trimming drapes, lamp shades, bedspreads, upholstery for chairs, and toilet seat covers, in case you made your own. They also suggested using rug braiding to make women's purses and sandals. The only tools required were rug braiders and a lacer.

Another handcrafted rug that is eagerly sought and quite expensive today is the Navajo woven rug. The Navajos are famous for their blankets, rugs, and saddle blankets. Some believe they learned the craft from the Pueblo Indians who learned how to make looms and weave from the Spaniards who brought the first sheep into Mexico. Actually the Navajos are more famous for their blankets than for their rugs. Indications are the latter was made on order while the blankets were made all the time. The blankets were used for a number of purposes like covering the opening of the wigwam or hogan, or wrapping around the body as a sleeping blanket.

Rugs were so essential in those cold New England homes the ladies used any craft they could master to make more and more rugs to cover the wooden floors. They had the yarn they had spun from the wool sheared from their own sheep so they began making knitted and crocheted rugs. They were perfect as the wool was warm and exactly what they needed. The materials were easy to acquire as the only thing needed other than the home grown wool was a crochet hook or a pair of knitting needles, both of which could easily be made at home. The tool maker didn't even have to be skilled, just able to whittle out two wooden knitting needles or a crochet hook.

Other types of handcrafted rugs known to have been made through the years are the tapestry or needlepoint rugs, the Turky Worke Carpetts, the cross stitch rugs, and the scalloped rug, also known as the tongue or petal rug. This one is very similar to the so-called penny rug. Then there are the very scarce handmade felt rugs, some covered in silk and wool embroidery. It has been said that the aborigines were the first to use felt, and it was the first textile to be used for floor covering. The advantages of making felt rugs was the fact they could be made quickly as the felt was already suited to floor covering. Not only was felt durable, it never frayed which meant the edges did not have to be finished unless the maker wanted to finish them. Felt rugs are not that popular today, probably due to their scarcity. They are seldom seen except at estate sales and even then not very frequently. When acquired, they are rarely used as rugs because most have beautiful embroidery and it seems a shame to walk on it. Not only did our ancestors stencil the walls of the house and the wood floors, they also stenciled oilcloth rugs. Some of these stenciled rugs were almost room size while others were only little 3 by 5 feet rugs.

Compared with a century ago, small numbers of all of these rugs are still being made today, and will probably continue to be made as long as people feel the need to make things with their hands. There are also antique examples that can be found from time to time. If for no other reason, they are very useful in keeping us in touch with our heritage.

Hooked rugs were and still are the most collectible of all old rugs. Popularity has influenced prices. $400-$500.

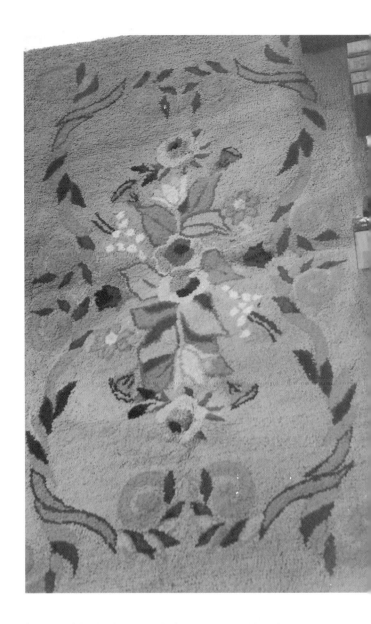

Center of hooked rug with floral design. $300-$400.

Felt rug embroidered with geometric design. $175-$225.

Close-up of needlework on rug.

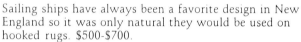

Sailing ships have always been a favorite design in New England so it was only natural they would be used on hooked rugs. $500-$700.

Our ancestors were noted for saving and utilizing everything. They saved small scraps of wool whether new or used, and used them to make rugs like this Petal example. Rugs made with round pieces were called Penny rugs. $75-$125.

Close-up of needlework on rug.

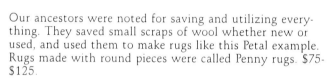

Another type of embroidered felt rug. $150-$200.

As proof that every type of material was used in rag rugs this one has a strip from an old pair of denim overalls. Again size and condition will determine prices. $50-$200.

Woven, wool rug believed to be American Indian-made. $100-$300.

Late Navajo rug. $75-$125.

They also made rag rugs in order to utilize every scrap and rag that could not be used elsewhere. Depending on size and condition, prices will vary from $50 to $200.

Braided rugs were also made originally of leftover scraps. They were and still are a favorite among both makers and users. Depending on size and condition prices can range from $100 to $1,000.

Needlepoint rug done with heavy yarn. $50-$100.

Our ancestors stenciled not only their walls and floors, they stenciled rugs to use on bare, unpainted floors. Prices will vary greatly for rugs in good condition, but generally they will run between $75 and $300 depending on size.

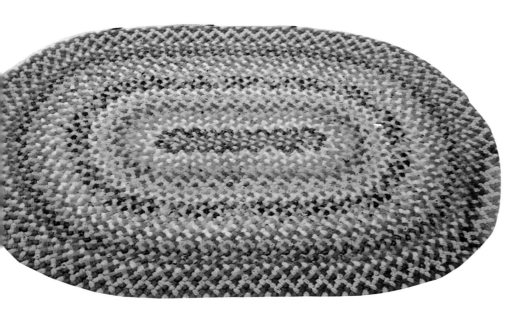

Families might have dozens of braided rugs like this.

Although braided rugs with hooked centers were made quite often in the past, they are very scarce today. $200-$300.

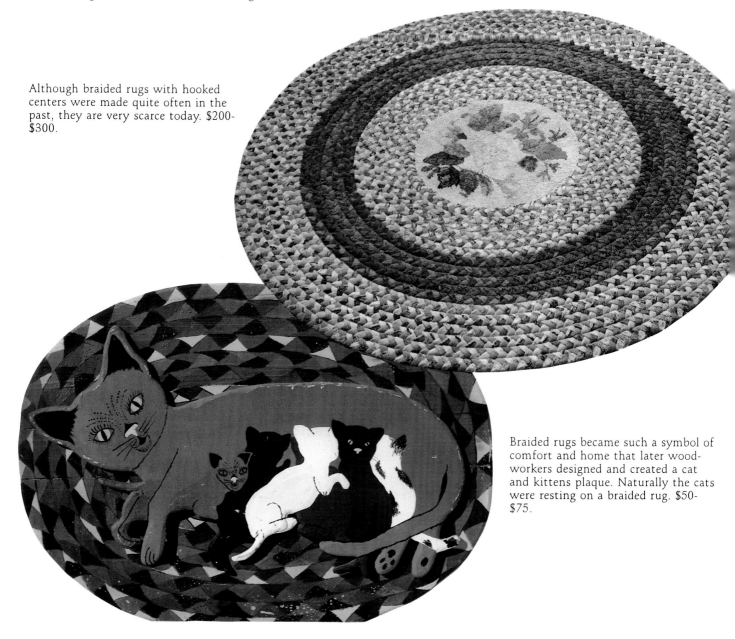

Braided rugs became such a symbol of comfort and home that later wood-workers designed and created a cat and kittens plaque. Naturally the cats were resting on a braided rug. $50-$75.

Crocheted granny squares were used to make this rug. Also suitable for bathroom. $15-$20.

Poorly made braided rug. Made either for rough use or was made by an amateur. $15-$20.

Small velour rug from the Orient. $25-$45.

Apparently this rug was crocheted out of leftover yarn. Fits nicely in small bathroom. $10-$15.

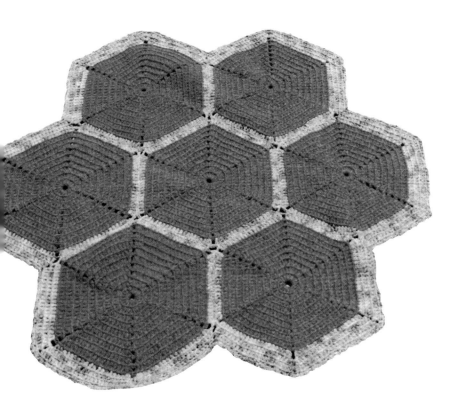

Crocheted rug using heavy rug yarn. $25-$30.

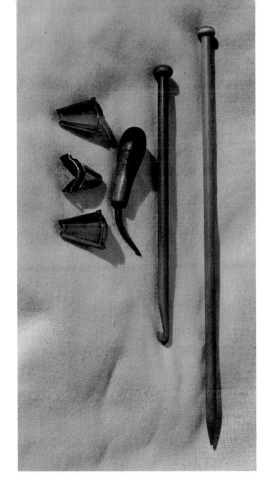

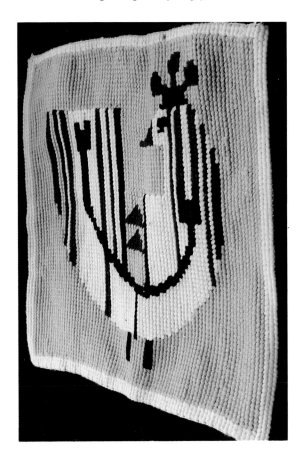

Tools used to make some of the rugs. Top shows folders for making the strips used in braiding a rug, next is curved hook for hooking rugs, and on the bottom are two large, wooden crochet hooks.

Later Latch Hook rugs became quite popular, both as a rug and as pick-up work for the homemaker. They can still be found at yard and garage sales at very reasonable prices. $5-$7.

Another late bloomer was the pieces done in needlepoint using heavy yarn. They could be framed and hung as pictures, or they could be used as small rugs. Still reasonably easy to find and inexpensive. $5-$8.

Chapter Eight
Scarves and Runners, Bureau, Piano, and Sideboard

For a century or more a little controversy has surrounded this category of linens. The first problem to arise was the choice of the title—should they be called scarves or runners? It was decided either could be used. Then there was the spelling, and it was found either the word scarfs or scarves was acceptable. The only problem we have now is trying to decide exactly what piece of furniture the piece was made for, provided we want to use it as it was used originally. However this problem is easy to solve as we can do exactly what the maker did—use it wherever it fits and looks best.

In 1927 an article on scarves suggested "It is the little finishing touches that give individuality and coziness" to homes. The author went on to say that "no matter how carefully and correctly the furniture may have been chosen, it is not until the accessories are arranged that a house is really a home. Much can be done with the scarfs and runners [even then both terms were being used] used on tables, dressers, buffets, etc., to either mar or complete a charming room." Four scarves or runners were shown along with directions for making each. A problem arose with the illustrations as one was square in shape. Old time needleworkers have a tendency to think of scarves or runners as being long and narrow. Centerpieces are square—or round. So, we are right back to the original solution—all needleworkers had and still have a tendency to make their household linens to fit their needs. If we collect the old pieces, then we have to use the same ingenuity. Chances are we are going to find a lot of scarves or runners in an eighteen by twenty seven inch size as it was described in the article as "being suitable for so many places," and they were used in so many places other than just the customary ones. For example, they were used in country homes on clock shelves as well as on the mantle. One had to be careful using the scarves on mantles, however, because if they were too wide and the mantle low there was a danger of fire.

Searching for scarves or runners can be most rewarding, as there are so many available. Because there are so many a problem can arise—which ones should we choose? The work on some pieces is absolutely exquisite. Drawn work is one example. Throughout the centuries this work has been known by such fascinating names as Hamburg Point, Opus Tiratum, Dresden Point, Broderie de Nancy, Tonder Point, and Ponto Tirato, but for the past century it has been known simply as drawn work. One of the reasons for the variety of earlier names was the fact all needlework began in the convents, originally done by the nuns and monks, and was primarily used on church linens and vestments. Then the nuns began taking in orphans whom they taught to do fine needlework. In the beginning they were very secretive

about needlework, but as time passed and more people learned how to make it, everybody began making beautiful linens. Perhaps the most interesting thing about drawn work is the fact that the same thread pulled or drawn from the fabric can be used to make the design, assuring the maker that it all matches.

Another beautiful type of needlework found on scarves and runners is Battenberg, also called Royal Battenberg or Renaissance lace. This is a rather late bloomer when we consider the fact that needlework has been made for centuries—and it is also an American creation, originated by New Yorker Sara Hadley somewhere around the last decade of the nineteenth century. Like so many other things in the needlework field, there is some question as to just how this work was named and for whom. There are those who think that since it was created about the time of the wedding of Princess Beatrice (youngest daughter of Queen Victoria) to Prince Henry it should be called Royal Battenberg. Others seemed to think it really got its name from the fact that Princess Beatrice did so much of this needlework after the death of her young husband. Regardless of exactly when the needlework was given its name, it seems this braid lace was definitely named for the Battenbergs. Compared to the amount of time required to make pillow or needle lace braid lace is fast and very attractive—not quite as attractive as the other laces, but very, very pretty indeed.

There are several things beginning collectors should know about Battenberg. First, many damaged pieces can be found and at very attractive prices. Examine the piece carefully. If the damage is more or less minor, it can be repaired. Using balls of thread found at estate sales and in some mall booths, thread that matches that which was used to make the piece, follow the exact stitching used on the good sections. This will require a little time, patience, and skill, but not nearly as much as was required of the original maker. In the end you will have a fine piece of Battenberg that probably didn't cost you over $10, if that much. At today's prices that piece repaired as perfectly as you can do would probably sell for $75 to $100, depending on the size and the quality.

Some scarves and runners will be found made entirely of crochet while others will have crocheted ends. The crocheted ends may have various birds and fowls, or they may have initials. There are also the plainer ones with tassels. Even though tatting was a slow and tedious type of needlework; nevertheless tatted scarves and runners can be found. Some will be done entirely in tatting while others may have tatted medallions. Probably the larger number of scarves and runners will be found with embroidery. They will be found done in white-on-white and in colors as bright as the rainbow. Few have been found lined although the author of the 1927 article on scarves suggested that "a lining of un-bleached muslin gives weight to the scarf and helps to hold it in position so that corners are not so easily turned up in that unsightly manner which is so annoying." Heavier fabrics were also used for linings. She went on to suggest that if the dining room table was small, a scarf might be used as a between-meals cover. It sounds like a lot of trouble to remove the cloth and put a scarf or runner on the table after a meal, but it was done half a century ago—by quite a few homemakers. They didn't have too much work to do, many had maids who performed this chore, and their home was their castle that they wanted kept just so.

Long scarf monogrammed on middle edge. Probably made originally for a sideboard. $14-$19.

The swastikas crocheted around the border of this scarf had an entirely different meaning in 1915 than it did in the thirties and forties. A 1913 card described it as a Good Luck Emblem. It went on to say, "The swastika is the oldest cross and emblem in the world. It forms a combination of four Ls standing for Luck, Light, Love, and Life." According to the card it dates back to 315 B.C. and has been found in use in all foreign countries as well as the Indian territories of the southwest. $25-$35.

Close-up of monogram.

60

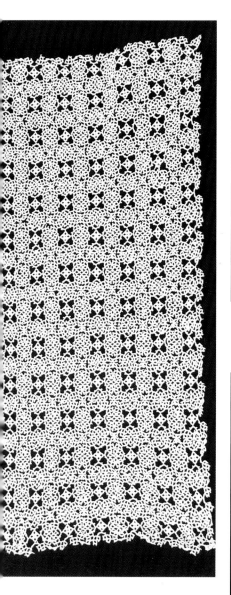

Small tatted scarf. $20-$25.

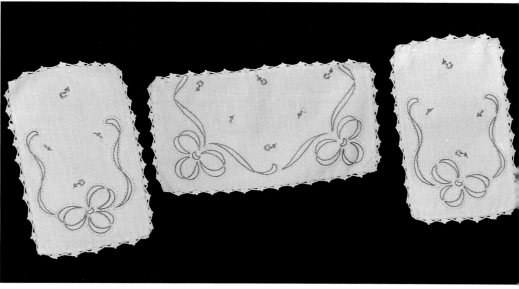

Another three piece that definitely appears to have been made originally for a vanity. $8-$12.

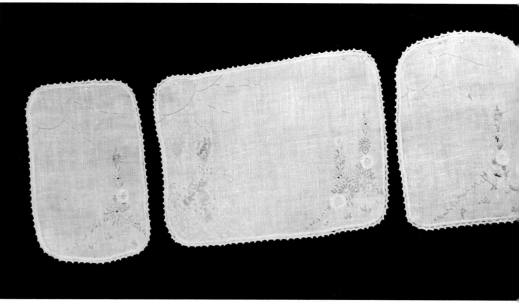

Three piece set could have been made for a dresser or a vanity. $8-$12.

Embroidered basket of flowers decorate either end of this scarf. Crocheted lace. $12-$15.

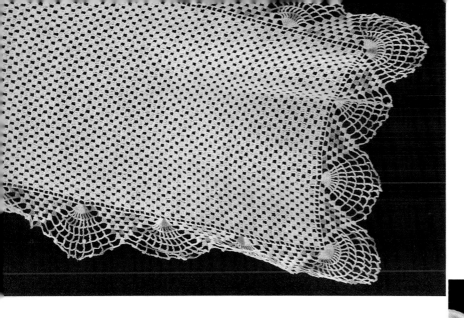

Crocheted white scarf with variegated border. $7-$10.

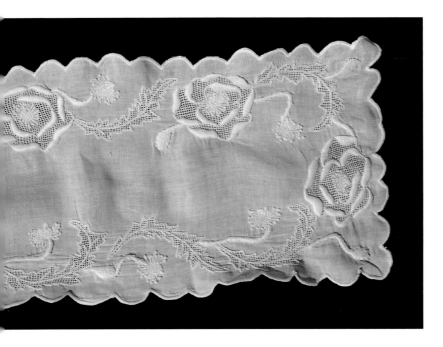

Heavily embroidered dresser scarf. $30-$35.

Close-up of center of scarf showing the work in more detail.

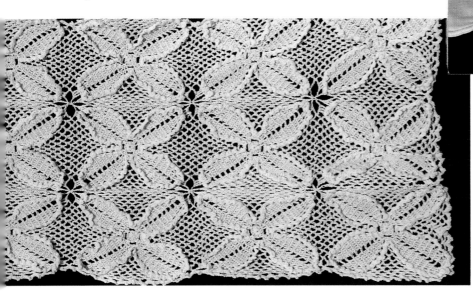

Unusual crocheted scarf. $15-$19.

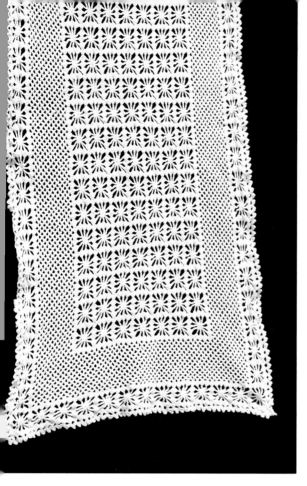

Crocheted scarf. $13-$16.

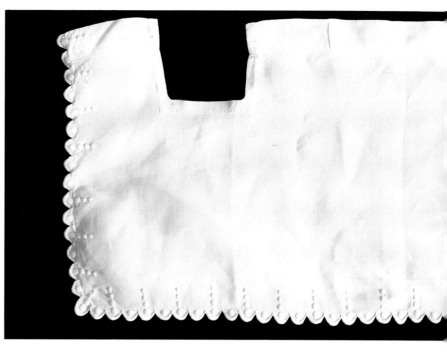

Scarves like this were made to fit Victorian dressers with small drawers on either side of the marble top. $18-$23.

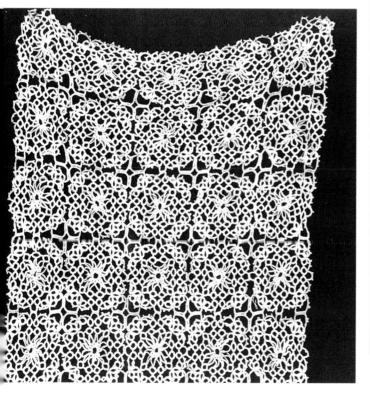

Varigated thread was used to tat this scarf. $12-$15.

Tassels and length would indicate this one was made to be used on a piano. $20-$25.

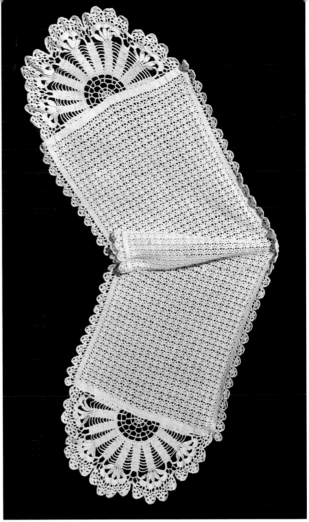

Scarf with flowers and scalloped border embroidered in yellow. $13-$18.

Crocheted scarf. $19-$23.

Close-up of one end.

Scarf with embroidered baskets of flowers on colored ground. $12-$16.

Same type scarf, different design. $9-$12.

Scarf with embroidery and fringe. $9-$12.

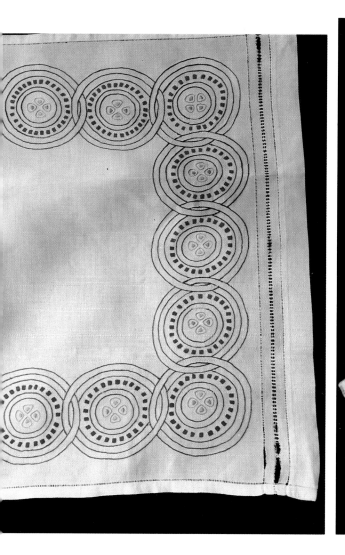

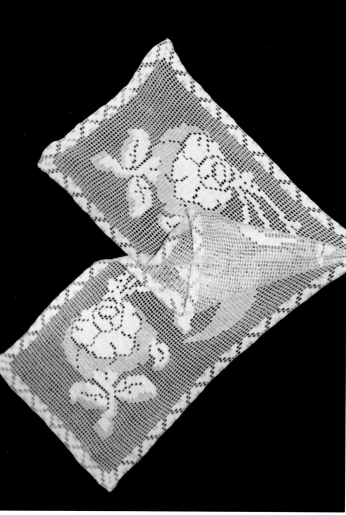

Extra wide scarf with design on only one end. $16-$20.

Crocheted scarf. $13-$16.

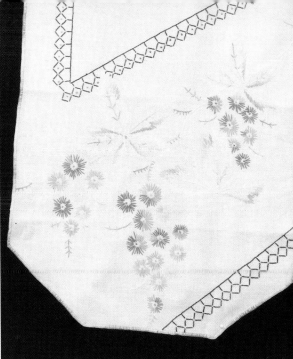

Ornate, overall cutwork scarf. Has some damage, probably done in ironing. As is $20-$25, perfect $35-$50.

Orange and black design embroidered on this scarf. $8-$13.

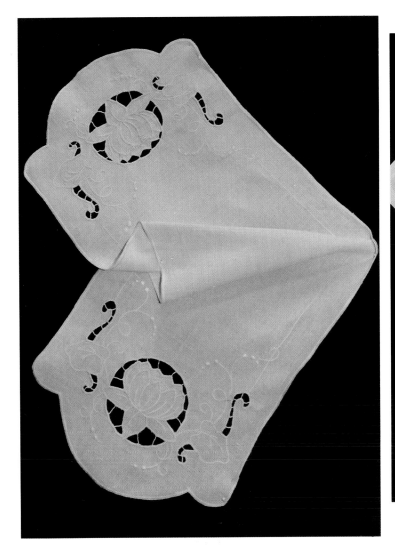

Scarf with cutwork design. $17-$25.

Scarf with cross stitch design. $13-$15.

Drawn work design decorated this scarf. $18-$24.

Late embroidered scarf. $8-$10.

Long scarf suitable for sideboard or piano. $20-$25.

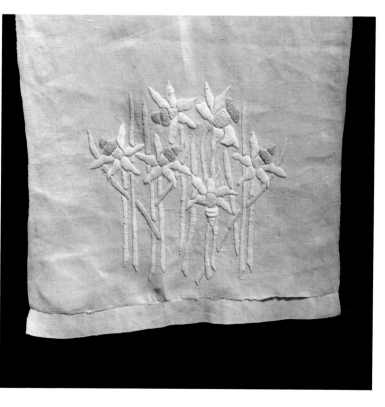

Scarf with crocheted insertion on either end. $13-$18.

Filet crocheted monogram on scarf. $15-$19.

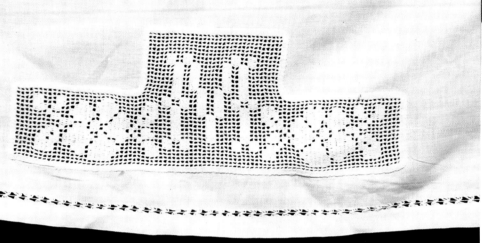

Close-up of monogram.

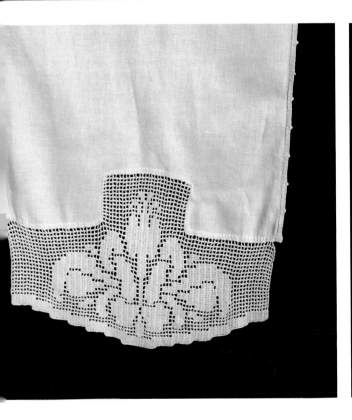

Scarves with crocheted ends were very popular. $12-$15.

Scarf designed and embroidered for cutwork yet never cut. $12-$15.

Close-up of the design.

A Sweet Dreams design was great for pillow cases, but not exactly appropriate for a dresser scarf, yet this was one of those cases where the maker used the design she wanted, apparently to make her bedroom linens match. $11-$16.

Close-up of the embroidery.

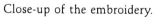

White-on-white embroidered dresser scarf. $18-$25.

Turkey red embroidery, drawn work, and fringe decorate this scarf. $23-$27.

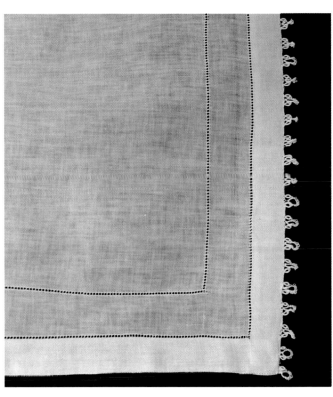

Hemstitched scarf with dainty, tatted lace. $10-$14.

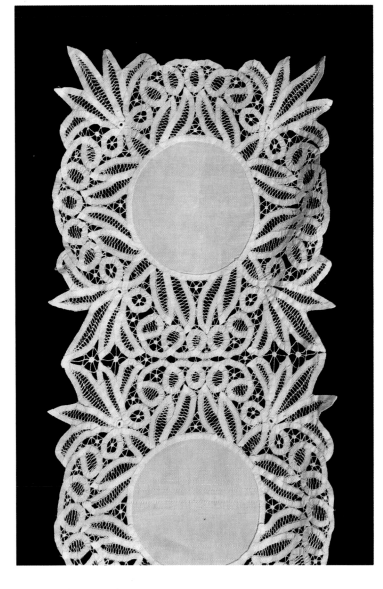

Battenberg scarf. $25-$35.

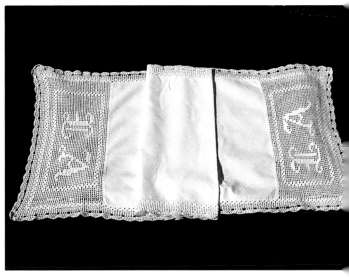

Long scarf with crocheted monogrammed ends. $20-$25.

Elegantly-done, white-on-white scarf. $28-$33.

Close-up of embroidery.

End of cutwork scarf done in pink. $20-$26.

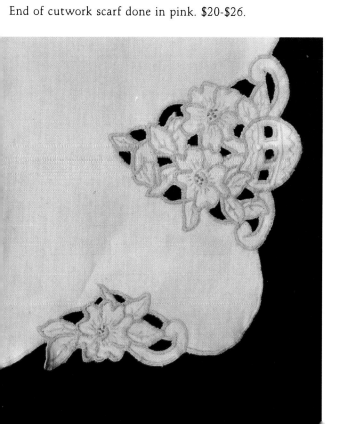

Scarf with dancing girls done in black cross stitch, crocheted lace. $12-$16.

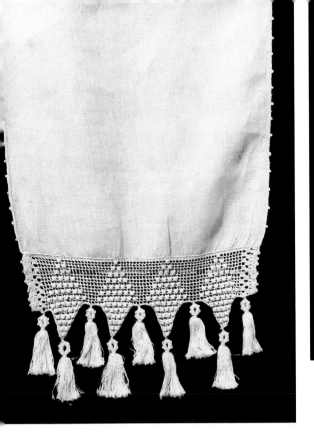

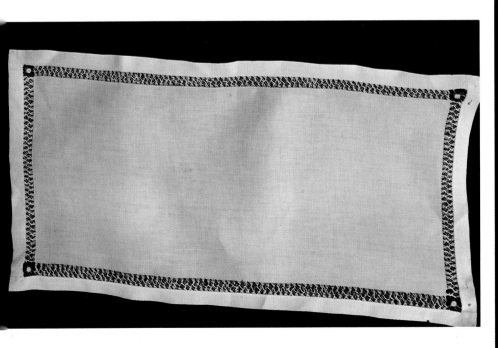

Scarf done in shades of pink and red cross stitch. $8-$12.

Extra length and tassels indicate piano scarf; although tassels were popular on dresser and sideboard scarves. $19-$23.

Crocheted scarf. $10-$15.

Scarf with one simple row of drawn work. $8-$12.

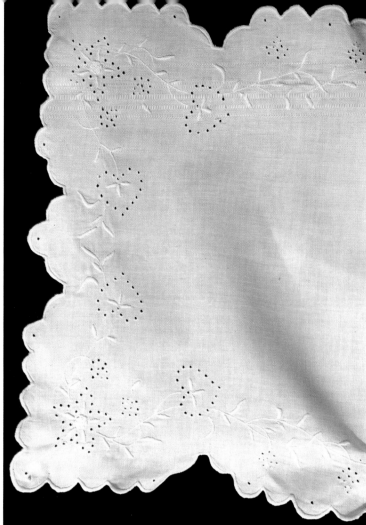

Ornate white-on-white embroidered dresser scarf. $17-$20.

Close-up of embroidery.

Drawn work could be used to make so many designs. $17-$24.

Machine-embroidered scarves like this were sold in dime stores in the fifties and sixties. $6-$9.

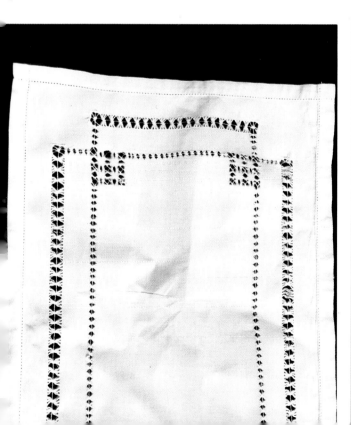

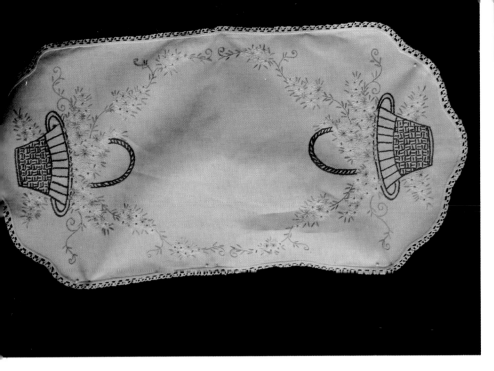

Scarf with embroidered design of basket and flowers. $12-$14.

Three rows of drawn work decorate this scarf. $16-$21.

Scarf with elaborate cutwork ends. $22-$27.

End of scarf with crocheted corners. $10-$15.

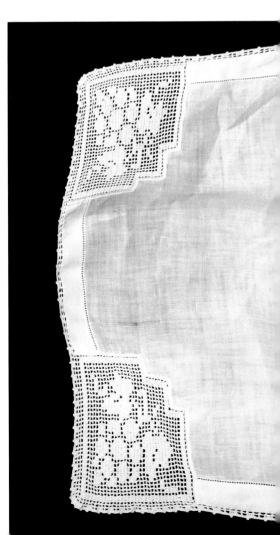

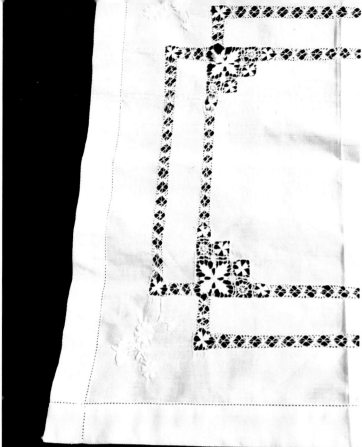

Another drawn work design. $15-$20.

Scarf with different crochet on either end. $15-$18.

Piano scarf with ornate drawn work design. $40-$50.

Close-up of end of scarf.

Scarf with cross stitched bouquet of flowers. $10-$12.

Dresser scarf with crocheted insertion on either end. $14-$18.

Long, narrow crocheted scarf probably for piano. $20-$26.

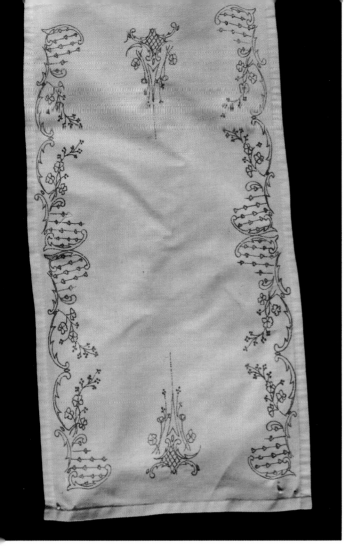

Hemstitched, white-on-white embroidered scarf. $23-$27.

Unusual design embroidered in turkey red thread. $12-$15.

End of embroidered scarf. $10-$12.

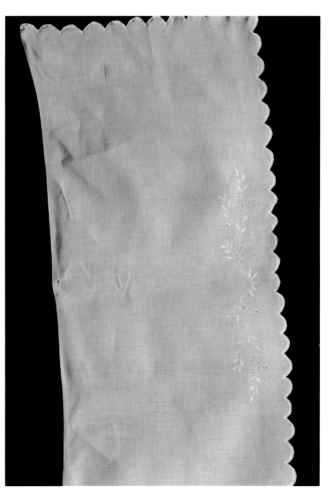

One side left plain would indicate this was probably made for a sideboard that remained against the wall. $15-$21.

Lined dresser scarf done in counted cross stitch. $30-$40.

Close-up of the colorful design.

Close-up of work on Battenberg scarf.

Old, very ornate Battenberg scarf. $75-$95.

Scarf with three letter monogram in filet crochet. $19-$23.

Long scarf with letter B in center. Probably for a sideboard. $25-$30.

Late Battenberg scarf. $20-$25.

Close-up of embroidery.

Another scarf with unhemmed sides. $9-$12.

Scarf with plain embroidery and unhemmed or selvedge edges. $9-$12.

Pastel colors were used to embroider this scarf. $9-$14.

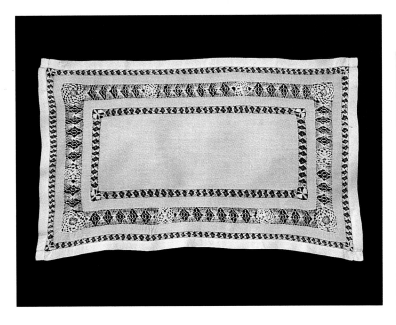

Short scarf with three rows of drawn work. $15-$20.

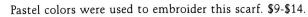

Late scarf with cornucopias embroidered in color. $8-$12.

Scarf with filet squares in each corner. $12-$15.

Scarf with design done in turkey red. $14-18.

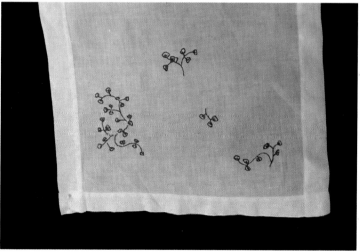

Scarf embroidered with dainty design done in turkey red thread. $15-19.

Embroidery on net. $23-$27.

Heavily embroidered scarf. $25-$30.

Late scarf with design cross stitched in colors. $9-$13.

Chapter Nine
Sheets and Blankets

It seems that sheets and blankets were one of those mundane things everybody just took for granted, until about 1850. It was about that time that women began to make fancy sheets, and later they would be monogrammed and have lace edgings. But in our research on their origin plenty of information has been found on beds, their placement in ancient homes, canopies, and mosquito netting, a very necessary evil as early as 3500 B.C. In those early days Egypt was so infested with mosquitoes, especially along the Nile, some of the commoners slept wrapped in their fishing nets at night. In other words the netting served a dual role—it was used for fishing during the day and to spread over the bed at night. But information on the actual sheet, when and where it was first made, what fabric was used early on, and any other pertinent information has escaped us completely. There was a mention of the ornately carved Roman beds which described them as "outfitted with expensive linens and silk," yet it failed to say whether the outfit was sheets, pillow cases, a canopy, or maybe a bedspread. Since most of the beds of the ancient world were described as being used for either sleeping at night, reclining during the day, or simply a place to stretch out while eating, it is a bit difficult to imagine them with fine sheets of any kind. But chances are they did have some, especially for those who could afford them.

Once women began making their feather mattresses there can be little doubt they also made sheets to cover them. These sheets might have been all linen, all cotton, or a mixture of linen and wool, the kind called linsey-woolsey that can still be found occasionally. The latter was made on looms at home until well into the 1950s in some areas. Since the fabric made on the home looms was never over three feet wide it had to be sewed together in the middle. There were no fitted sheets at that time and the majority of home loomed flat sheets didn't hang too far over the sides of the bed, oftentimes not even enough to tuck under the mattress. The seam down the middle usually kept the two occupants on their respective sides of the bed. There was another type of sheet that made for miserable sleeping, and that was the kind many farm families made out of hundred pound feed and flour sacks or bags. After the bags were emptied, the stitching was taken out of the side and bottom. The bags were washed and bleached until they were snowy white, then four were sewn together. There was durability in those heavy sheets, and there was also a bulky seam. This writer remembers well spending the night with a little girl from grammar school. She had sheets made of feed sacks on her bed, and that seam around the hips left a lasting memory.

An exact date for when the ready-made sheet first appeared on the market is unknown. It is known that most affluent families had maids who also doubled as seamstresses, or if the family was large they might have a full-time seamstress. Not only did they make much of the clothes worn by the family, they also did any other sewing that was necessary—like hemming sheets. No mention was made of ready-made sheets in Jordon Marsh's 1891 catalog, but they did offer linen sheeting in several widths. In the catalog it was described as "Our stock of linen sheetings and of pillow case linens is unusually large, and comprises of the very best makes of Scotch, German, Belgian, Barnsley, and Irish goods." Prices ranged from 87.5 cents a yard for two yard wide sheeting to $3 for three yard wide piece. In the less affluent and farm families the homemaker did most of the sewing, including making the sheets that might be made of muslin or other suitable fabric.

Some of those latter sheets can be found monogrammed and with factory-made or homemade lace. Others will be found with beautifully embroidered designs. Antique dealers who specialize in linens will usually have some, and they can still be found sometimes in estate sales.

A sheet in any color other than white was unthinkable until after World War II, when colors seem to blossom out. Kitchen appliances and bathroom fixtures were also being offered in several colors. By the sixties floral sheets were making their appearance in the stores and on the beds of American homes. Rather than expect the homemaker to embroider her own sheets, the manufacturers began offering sheets with embroidered borders. Fieldcrest was a leader in this new trend. Many of the people who worked in the Pepperell mills in Maine were able to buy sheets and pillow cases at reduced prices in the fifties and sixties. They stored them in their attics and barns, and when they are preparing to leave these homes now they will offer the sheets and cases at yard or barn sales so it is still possible to get the fine, old percale sheets and cases that were made thirty and forty years ago.

Blankets are not nearly as plentiful which makes them much harder to find. It's understandable when we remember each bed had at least two sheets while only one blanket may have been used, and then only in winter. In most areas quilts were much more popular than blankets, probably for several reasons. Not everybody had sheep, so obtaining wool for a blanket could be a problem. Some families preferred quilts saying they were warmer than blankets, and then there were those who felt it was frugal to use all the tiny scraps of fabric for quiltmaking. But there were blankets, both the factory-made and the home-loomed. In the forties and fifties as the women went to work outside the home they didn't have time to make quilts so blankets became more popular. In fact, lots of plaid blankets, usually not all wool, appeared on the market. Then there were the all-wools in solid colors. As far as is known there is little demand for the old blankets today, even when found. Reports have come in that a few people are using the old, wool, plaid ones to make winter jackets. This is a novel idea and they should make up into a warm and very attractive jacket. The old wool blankets that were loomed at home can still be found now and then. They are easy to recognize as they have a seam right down the middle. The old loom could only weave a three foot wide strip so two had to be made for each blanket. Some will have colorful woven borders while most will have a blanket stitch or other fancy stitch across the ends where a hem has been turned under.

Embroidered and monogrammed sheets originated with the Victorians. $25-$30.

Floral sheets were becoming very popular by the sixties. $5-$7.

Factory-embroidered duvet. Some can be filled with down while others hold blankets. Popularity has increased during past decade. $45-$65.

Later sheet with less embroidery. $13-$18.

By the early seventies big floral sheets were very popular. $5-$8.

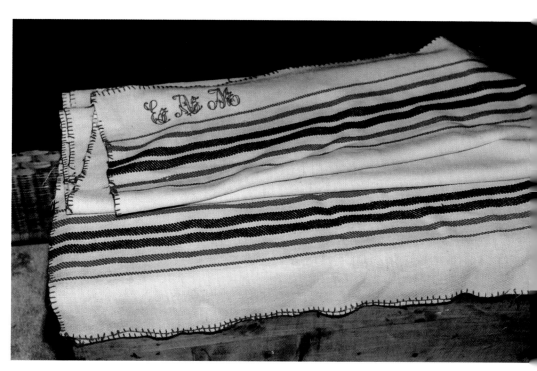

Matching linen sheet and pillow case with knitted lace, hemstitched, and name *Purdy* embroidered on both. $50-$75 for pair.

All-wool blankets were also woven on the home looms. Yarn was dyed to make the stripes. Apparently the maker was very proud of her work as she embroidered her initials on the top. Also blanket stitched around the top, bottom, and sides. $75-$125.

Also during the sixties factory-embroidered borders on sheets were becoming plentiful. $6-$9.

Home woven wool blanket with red and yellow stripes. $85-$110.

Close-up showing how the blanket was put together.

Linsey-woolsey sheets were woven on home looms using a combination of linen thread and wool yarn, hence the name. Made in two pieces and then sewn together. Fancy stitchery on either end. Rather scarce now. $45-$65.

Home woven wool blanket with stripes in assorted colors. Same colors used to blanket-stitch the ends. Note seam where blanket was put together. $80-$95.

Chapter Ten
Tablecloths—Large, Small, and In-between

As far as is known, no one has made a study of the number of household linens made in each category, but an educated guess would put the tablecloth at the top of the list. Every household had numerous tables and the ladies made stacks of cloths to fit each. The cloth for the big dining room table was probably the most important and generally plainer. In fact, more large damask tablecloths will be found than any other kind. Part of the popularity could probably be attributed to the magazine articles praising "The Noble Tradition of Linen Damask." An article in *Country Life* from 1927 declared that damask was still the most sought after material for tablecloths in conservative households—just as it had always been. The writer attributed much of the success of damask to the designs in it, designs that were executed by fine artists, they said. The best and most sought after designs, they said, were the Chippendale and Adams which followed the furniture designs of both of those famous furniture makers. Another popular pattern was the Willow which matched the popular china that depicted scenes from the ancient Chinese fable. It was also said that British damask designers did not hesitate to go to other countries for ideas, and that accounts for the fleur-de-lis pattern as well as several others. It is not unusual today to find old damask tablecloths with gorgeous designs, especially floral ones. Occasionally one will be found with a monogram and then there are the later cutwork and Battenberg Lace cloths, but the older damask ones are usually quite plain. Some of the most exquisite old cloths are the linens with drawn work and embroidery, always white on white. During the early part of this century Bucilla and other companies began offering large, stamped, linen cloths ready for embroidery, a trend that continues, but on a much smaller scale.

Chances are slim that the average collector will find many old pieces of needlework made in other countries, but there is an abundance of pieces from Japan and the Philippines that are fifty years old and older. There may even be some old pieces made in China, but there is an abundance of new needlework coming in from China, and has been for a decade or so. Much fine embroidery was made in Cuba a century ago, but it was done primarily on underwear and gowns for the affluent bride's trousseau. During the Korean War many of the servicemen sent embroidered, especially cut work, tablecloths and napkins home to their wives, and sometimes all their families and neighbors. They were beautifully done and not too expensive. I still have a banquet size, cut work tablecloth with twelve matching napkins that I asked a relative to send me during that time. Of course I refunded the money it had cost him for both the cloth, napkins, and postage. The total was less than $15. Since my mother made most of our clothes and all the household linens, there was great excitement in our home when she bought us muslin or nainsook underwear that usually had a label describing it as "Guaranteed Philippine Embroidery." And once in a while she might see a tablecloth or pillow cases with the same label and buy them. These are the pieces collectors are most likely to find today.

To understand this obsession with tablecloths we have to go back to some of the first homes in America. Those first homes might only consist of two rooms, but since they had to eat, they would have a board that could be put on a stand or frame to serve as a table or trestle. As soon as they were able to grow enough flax for a bit of extra fabric they began making cloths for those boards, cloths they called boardcloths. By the late 1600s girls from the more affluent families were making boardcloths or tablecloths for their dower chest. By the middle 1800s no one, except for the poorest of people, thought of eating on a bare table. Everybody used tablecloths. This custom continued well into this century.

It is believed that the introduction of the so-called breakfast nook in the twenties signaled the beginning of the place mats and napkins. Prior to that time many families had had small tables in the kitchen or a small hall where the family might eat breakfast—two or three at a time, but even this table was covered with a good tablecloth. The family might eat breakfast or even lunch a few at a time, but the entire family was required to gather around the big dining room table for dinner at night. These breakfast nooks or booths began to be built into the house, as a separate room, and some still used small tablecloths but they were beginning to use place mats more and more. By this time most families were much smaller than they had been previously so this arrangement worked well. And if place mats and napkins were acceptable in the breakfast nook, they would fit well on the dining table for the smaller families. So, the ladies began embroidering, crocheting, and tatting place mats with long matching runners for the center of the table.

One of the most interesting things about our tablecloth research has been the fact they were so seldom mentioned. A few old wills and inventories listed cubberd cloths, but this was for the cupboard not the table. One old will dating back to the 1700s listed a boardcloth. It is also known their use was not widespread until around 1775 or later, but tablecloths were not even mentioned in these later wills and inventories. About the middle of the eighteenth century one prosperous New England farmer remembered in his will his "dearly beloved wife" to whom he left a slave, cattle, a riding horse, a feather bed, pewter, silver, and fabric consisting of a "piece of Camblitt" to make a cloak, a "piece of worsted," and a "linnen wheel and a woollen wheel" apparently to make her own fabric for mundane things like tablecloths, if she used them.

According to many of the magazines a new type of tablecloth burst upon the scene around the twenties, and that was the bridge tablecloth. Bridge was probably the newest and most popular card game in the country. Etiquette decreed every table be covered with a cloth, and when a couple had friends over for bridge and refreshments they might use as many as half a dozen tables—or more. In a 1934 issue of *Needlecraft* one lady wrote "The serving of bridge-table refreshments having become so universally popular, today's hostess needs to be well fortified with many sets of small linens if her mind is to be at ease during the season of mid-winter entertaining. These small cloths are usually made of thirty-six inch material and the accompanying napkins are twelve inches in size." Although by this late date tablecloths of all kinds could be bought ready made, nevertheless it is easy to find in at least one issue of each needlework magazine each year instructions for making some kind of tablecloth, usually one associated with bridge and refreshments.

In 1925 they were calling them card-table covers and were giving all kinds of instructions for making the covers as well as menus for "bridge-suppers." One writer insisted the embroidery be simple so as not to interfere with the handling of the cards. She also suggested the cloths or covers be made in a neutral color because a white cloth under a brilliant light could be very trying on the eyes. A surface sheen could be tiring while black or any bright color "is not a pleasant selection." She offered three menus for bridge-suppers along with details on preparation. The first menu suggested baked ham, escalloped potatoes, jellied apple salad, rolls, coconut cake, and coffee. The second was chipped beef croquettes, green peas, pickled beets, hot biscuits, apple pie a la mode, and coffee while the third recommended creamed chicken, corn pudding, bread and butter sandwiches, olives and pickles, ice cream, and coffee.

Then as now people had different opinions, and four years later in 1929 another article in *Needlecraft* contradicted the earlier one against using black fabric or one with a sheen. Actually, this writer stressed the importance of using black sateen by saying, "It gives the smooth playing surface so much desired by bridge enthusiasts—a surface that is not slippery yet one on which the cards will not stick." Black sateen was also described as easy to decorate and easy to launder. Another article suggested making and giving bridge tablecloths as gifts for either birthdays or Christmas. Believe it or not they didn't suggest giving just one, but said that three cloths made a nice gift. This will probably help account for the number of bridge cloths still available today. The only other household linens made and given in such quantity were towels and pillow cases.

Other tablecloths were made in a variety of sizes—apparently to fit wherever they were needed. We also have to remember there were furniture makers, called turners because they turned out the various pieces, in every neighborhood. They made pieces to the housewife's specifications, if her husband couldn't make it. This means there were quite a few tables that didn't fit the usual mold. Cloths were made to fit them—whatever it took. Collectors today sometimes have problems trying to decide exactly what certain cloths were made to fit. We had this experience recently. An antique dealer had a box of linens she had bought from an estate, and she told us we could buy any of them although she had not had time to price or label them. Since our favorite in old linens is turkey red embroidery and gorgeous old white-on-white embroidery, we chose all those pieces. The two pieces done in turkey red were actually tea cart covers, but when the dealer made our bill they were listed and priced as tablecloths.

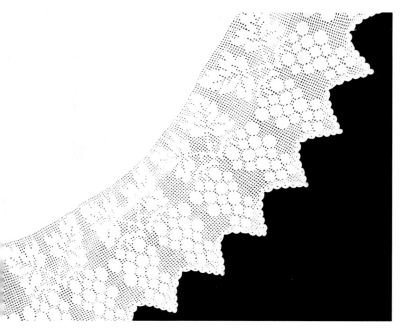

Round tablecloth with wide crocheted lace. $35-$50.

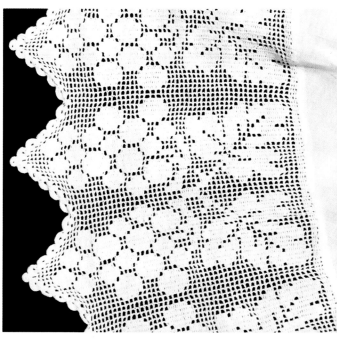

Close-up of the lace.

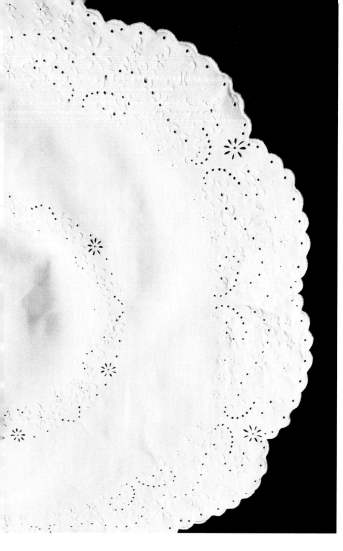

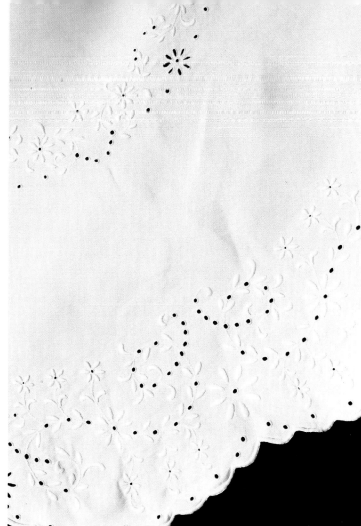

Heavily embroidered round, linen tablecloth. $35-$50.

Close-up of the embroidery.

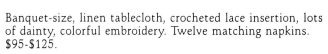

Banquet-size, linen tablecloth, crocheted lace insertion, lots of dainty, colorful embroidery. Twelve matching napkins. $95-$125.

Close-up of the design and the work.

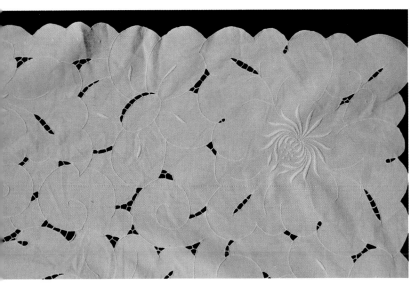

Embroidered and cutwork tablecloths like this were sent home during the Korean War. Twelve matching napkins. $95-$125.

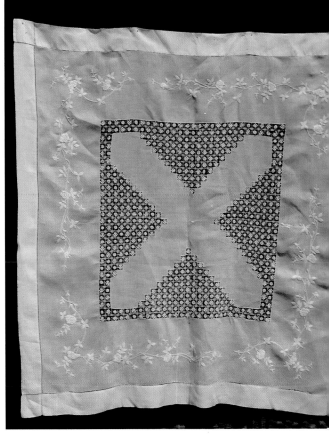

Drawnwork and embroidery decorated cloth. $30-$40.

Close-up of the work.

Ornate cutwork tablecloth. $95-$110.

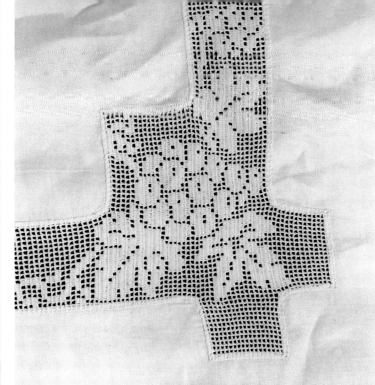

Center of this tablecloth has insertion of crocheted grapes and leaves. $50-$75.

Close-up of crocheted design.

Linen and lace tablecloth from the fifties and sixties. $75-$95.

Smaller, less ornate Battenberg tablecloth also has linen center with drawn work design. $35-$45.

Elegant, smaller Battenberg tablecloth, embroidered linen center. $45-$65.

Crocheted tablecloth. $29-$36.

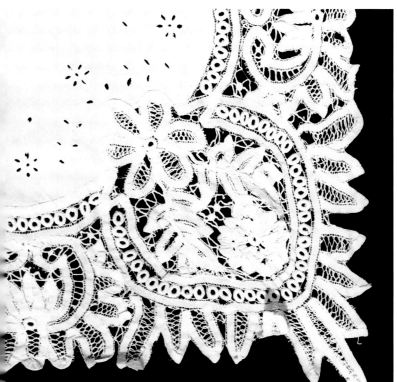

Close-up of the design.

Factory-made, round, tapestry-like tablecloth from the twenties. $30-$40.

Round linen tablecloth with pink cross stitch design. $19-$24.

Heavy lace tablecloth popular in the thirties. One like this sold recently in our area for $250.

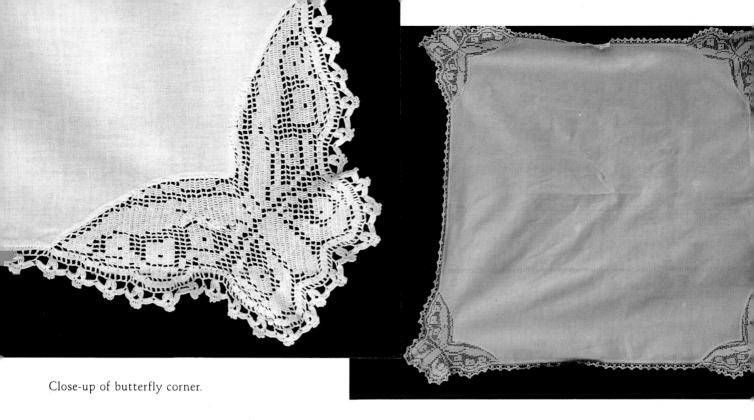

Close-up of butterfly corner.

Small cloth ideal for card table suppers before the bridge game. Filet crochet corners. $25-$30.

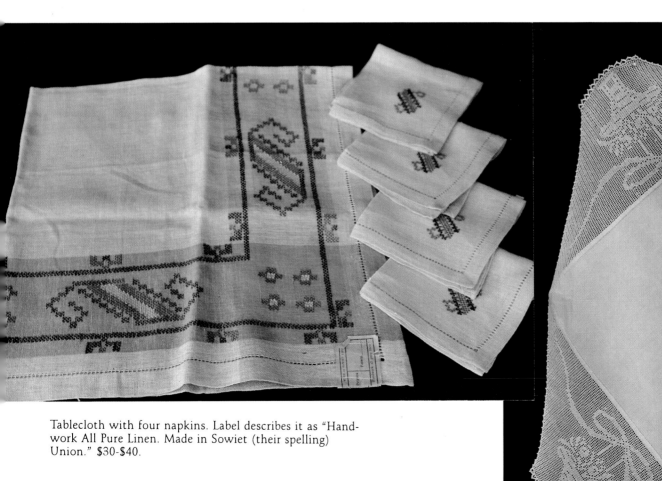

Tablecloth with four napkins. Label describes it as "Handwork All Pure Linen. Made in Sowiet (their spelling) Union." $30-$40.

Small cloth with baskets of flowers crocheted in the corners. $19-24.

Tablecloth embroidered in shades of blue. $25-$31.

Close-up of design.

Hemstitched linen cloth with crocheted lace. $17-$21.

Small, bordered tablecloth with basically cross stitch design. $18-24.

Two of a set of six crocheted placemats with matching table runner. $35-$40 for complete set.

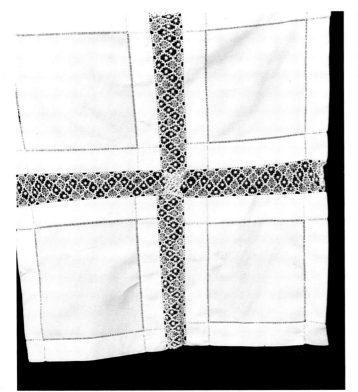

Four hemstitched squares were put together to form this small cloth. $20-$24.

Close-up of the unusual use of rick rack and Battenberg stitches to form the center panel to hold squares in above tablecloth.

The ever popular red checked damask tablecloth and napkins. $15-$20.

Large linen tablecloth embroidered with bouquets of violets. Twelve matching napkins. $85-$100 for the set.

Close-up of center design.

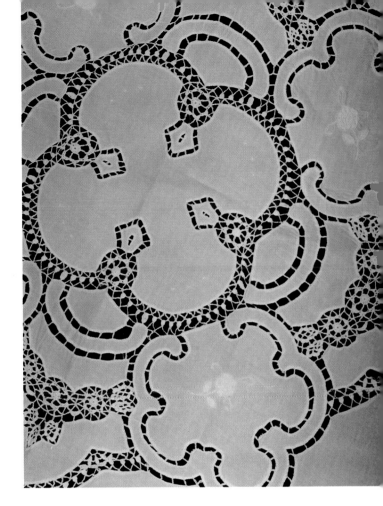

Embroidery, crochet, and cutwork were combined in this tablecloth. $50-$75.

Close-up of the design.

Grapes on table covered with a Battenberg cloth.

The teapot, creamer, and sugar dish crocheted in the corner of this cloth left little doubt it was made to be used on the tea table. $16-$23.

The use of china in the same colors as the embroidery shows how attractive a table can be.

Checkered damask cloths were used later with simple tea services.

Brown tablecloth with appliquéd fall leaves. $18-$23.

Pale green and blue embroidery decorates this cloth, crocheted lace. $19-$24.

Tea tables were always covered with a lovely tablecloth.

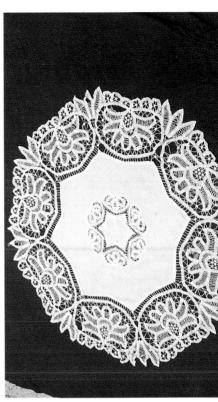

Round Battenberg tablecloth. $45-$65.

Round, brown tablecloth with appliquéd design. Six napkins. $20-$25.

Very unusual drawn work tablecloth, probably designed by the maker. $100-$125.

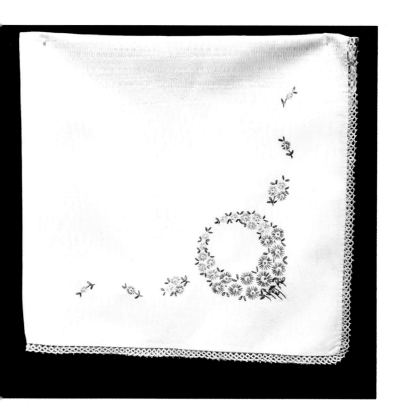

Cloth with flowers and tatted lace. $16-$19.

Silky lace tablecloth. $30-$40.

Interesting cloth as part of the pattern was designed to hold a napkin in each corner. $17-$21.

Corner is as attractive with as without the napkin.

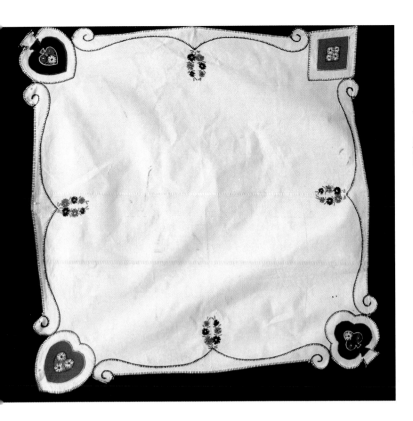

Bridge cloth with appliquéd and embroidered design. $15-$20.

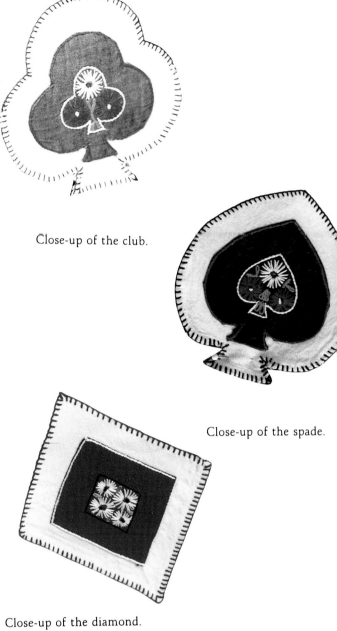

Close-up of the club.

Close-up of the spade.

Close-up of the diamond.

Bridge cloths are easy to identify as so many have the designs from the cards. Ties on the corners held them secure. $10-$12.

Close-up of the corner with the heart design.

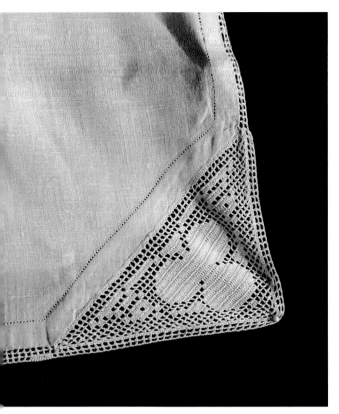

Close-up of the filet crocheted club.

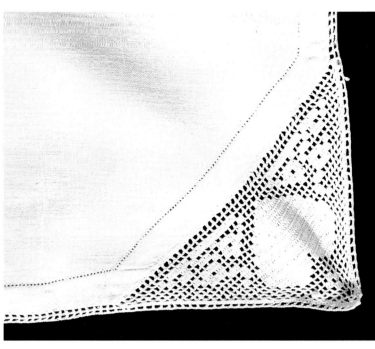

Close-up of the heart.

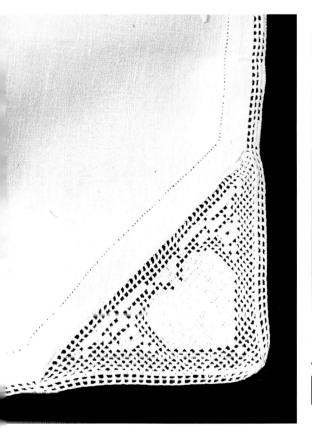

-up of the spade.

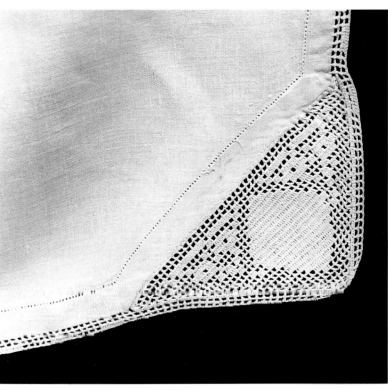

Close-up of the diamond.

Corner of small tablecloth showing the embroidery. $15-$19.

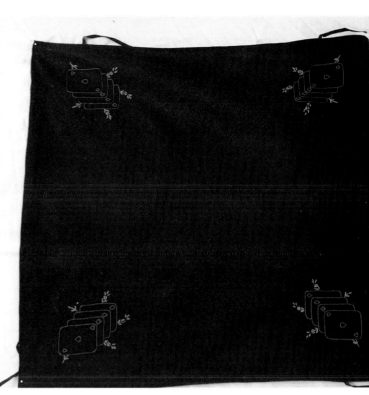

Many magazine articles recommended using black sateen for bridge cloths. $18-$22.

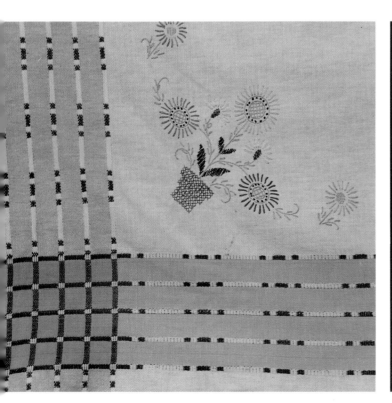

Corner of a tablecloth showing the design. $17-$19.

Corner of cloth showing embroidery.

Tablecloth with ornate cutwork design. $40-$50.

Close-up of the cutwork in the center.

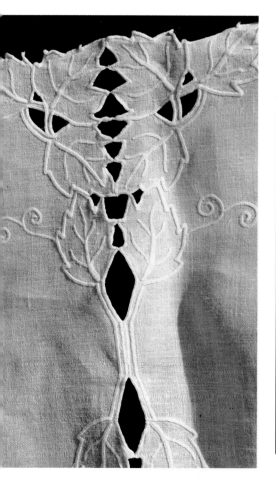

Close-up of bottom.

Small linen cloth with crocheted corners. Four matching napkins. $23-$29.

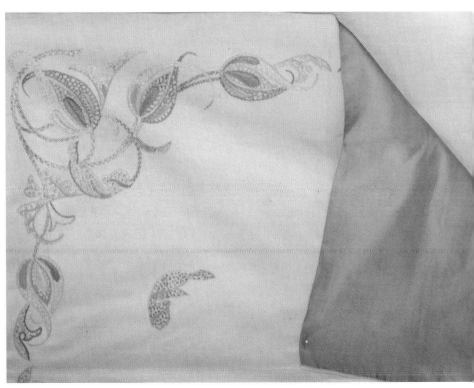

Heavily embroidered tablecloth. Lined with gold colored fabric. $25-$29.

Close-up of embroidery and lining.

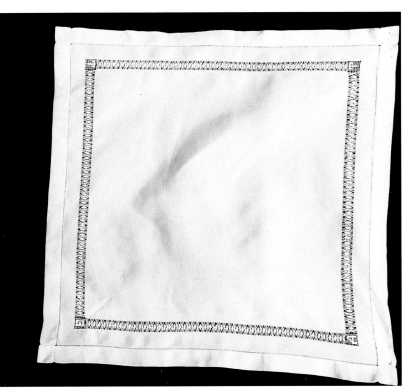

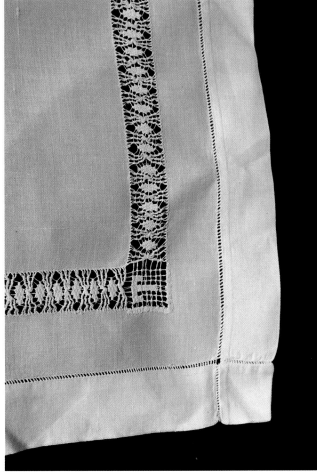

Small tablecloth with drawn work and initials in corner. $16-$21.

Close-up of the work.

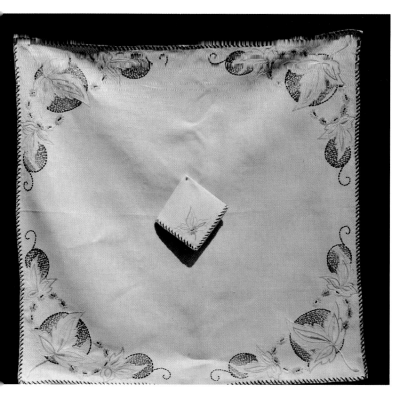

Embroidered cloth with four matching napkins. $17-$22.

Close-up of the design.

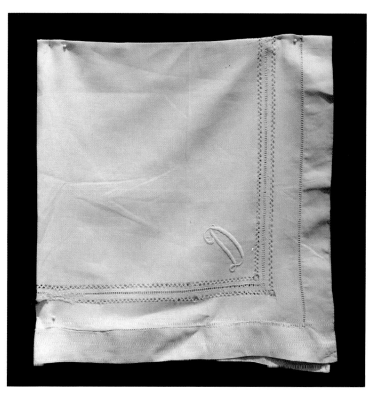

r of large damask tablecloth, hemstitched, drawn and one initial monogram. $40-$50.

Small tablecloth with drawn work and monogram. $16-$20.

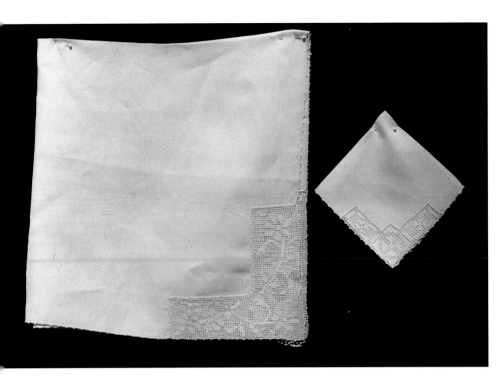

Small tablecloth with crocheted corners and matching napkins. $25-$30.

Small tablecloth with three-letter monogram. $14-$17.

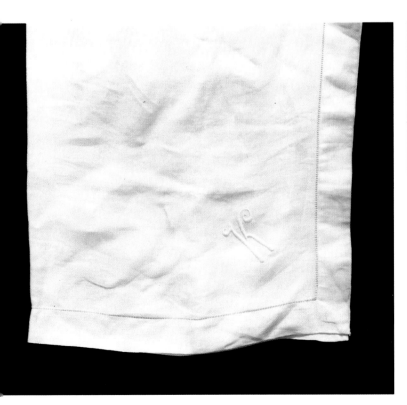

Small monogrammed tablecloth. $12-$15.

Small linen tablecloth with crocheted lace. $13-$19.

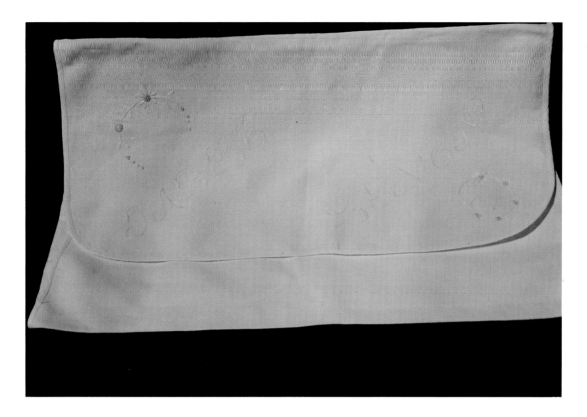

Storage bags were made for practically every use. Generally the name of the item to be stored was embroidered on the top. In this case it is *Table* and *Linen*. $10-$15.

Close-up of the embroidered word table.

Close-up of the word linen.

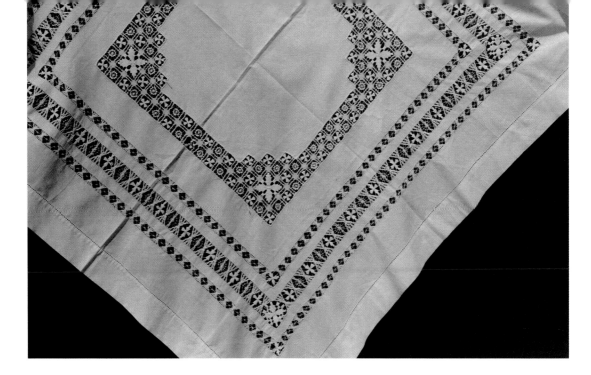

Almost as much of this tablecloth is covered in drawn work as is left plain. $55-$85.

Another view of the cloth.

Close-up of the design.

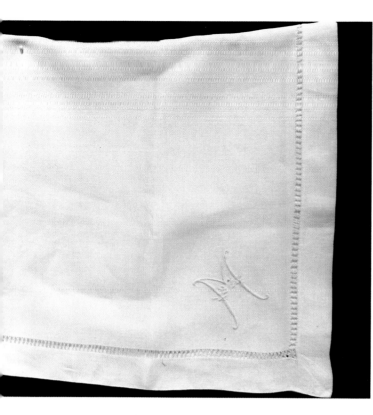

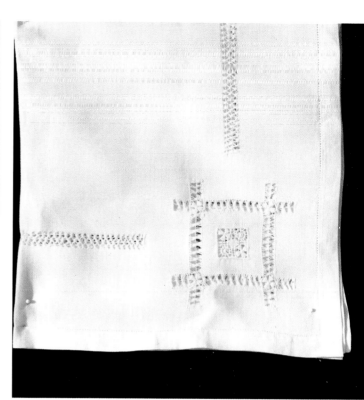

Small, simple tablecloth with single letter monogram. $10-$12.

Small tablecloth with drawn work. $19-$24.

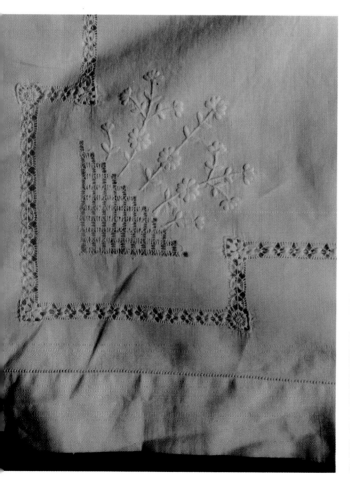

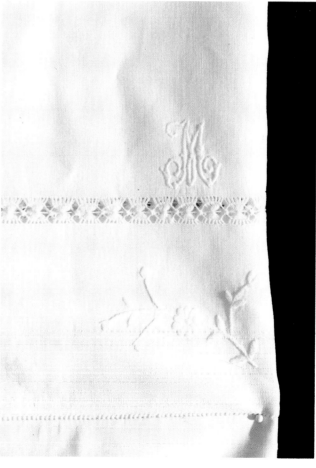

Corner of beautifully designed tablecloth. $40-$60.

Same cloth showing more of the design.

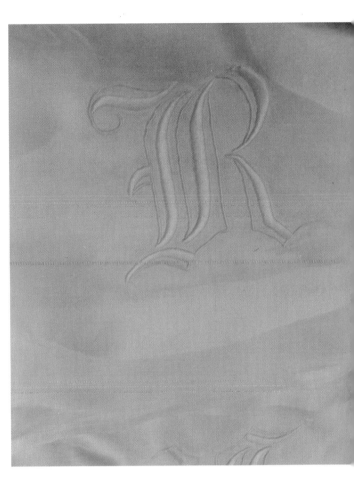

Black sateen bridge cloth with floral design done in silk thread. $15-$19.

Large damask tablecloth, only decoration is large, heavily embroidered R on either side. Eight matching napkins. $75-$95.

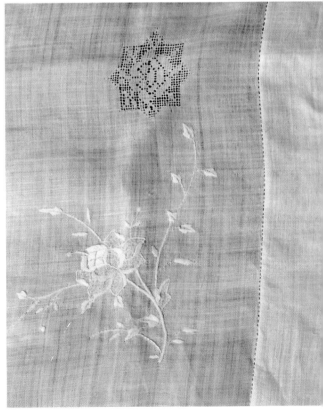

Cloth made of Canton linen, also called grass cloth, Chinese grass cloth, and grass linen. Probably made in China before the forties. $40-$50.

Embroidered tablecloth. $19-$24.

Small tablecloth with drawn work in the corners. $20-$26.

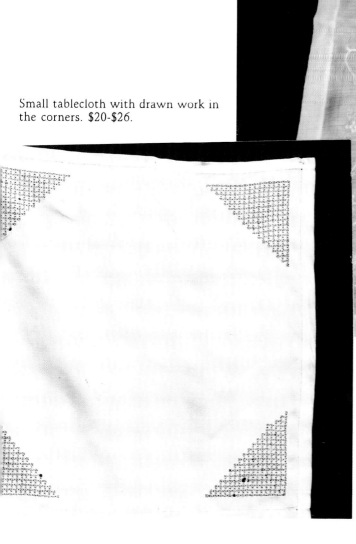

Tablecloth probably embroidered in China or the Philippines in the forties. $30-$40.

Close-up of the embroidery.

Holiday tablecloth embroidered with brown and gold thread. $20-$25.

Small linen tablecloth with three letter monogram and drawn work. $22-$28.

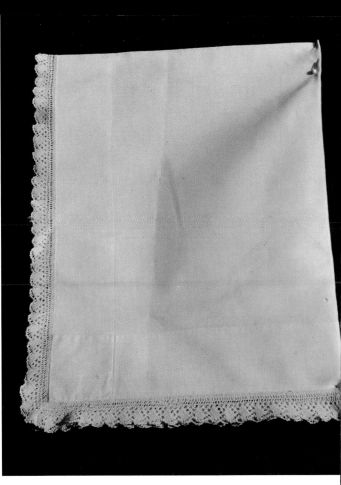

Small linen tablecloth with deep hem and crocheted lace. $23-$29.

Tablecloth with embroidery and drawn work. $40-$55.

Damask tablecloth with letters L and F on either side, tatted lace. $30-$35.

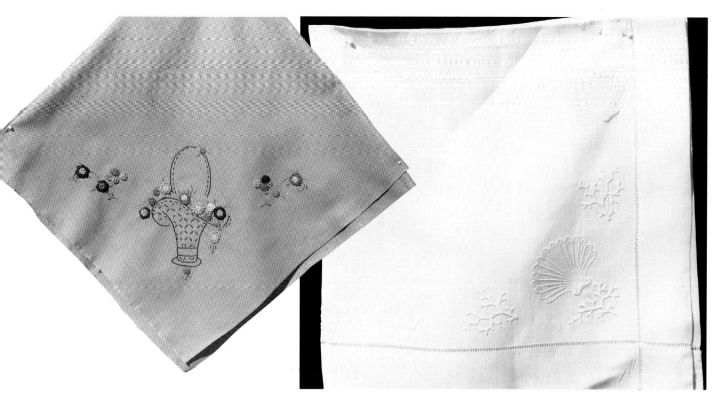

Small pink tablecloth with embroidered flowers and basket. $15-$17.

Sea motif was embroidered on this small tablecloth. $17-$23.

Rather plain, small tablecloth. $12-$15.

Tablecloth with embroidery and crocheted lace. $20-$25.

Crocheted tablecloth for small oblong table. $23-$29.

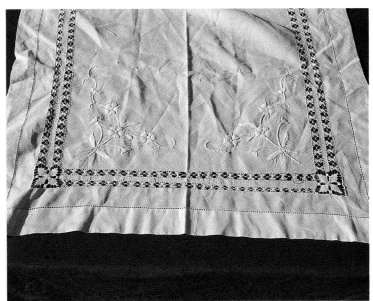

Tablecloth with drawn work and embroidery. $50-$75.

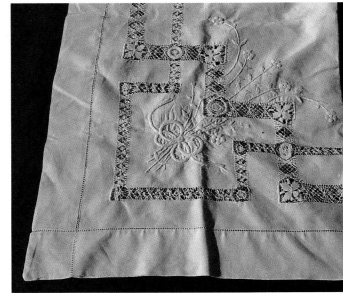

Corner of ornate tablecloth with lots of embroidery and drawn work. $85-$100.

Chapter Eleven
Towels and Splashers

Towels have always been popular, but probably never as popular as they were in the days when there was no bathroom in the house. Of course some homes have had bathrooms since the mid-1800s, even in the farm areas, when some wealthy planters designed tanks on the top of the house to hold rain water that could be heated by the sun and used for bathing. Tin and tin lined tubs were famous in the old west, but they were not stationary or built-in as some of the later tin-lined tubs were. Bathrooms have been installed and used in the cities for well over a century, in some areas for even longer, then there are some areas still using their outhouses or privies today. A recent article in a Portland, Maine, newspaper stated there were 19,000 outhouses still in use in the state of Maine. But the popularity of the towel did not depend on whether or not the home had a privy, it depended on whether or not bathing was done in a tub or in a bowl. In the days before the installation of a bathtub family and guests depended on a pitcher of water and a bowl for their bath. The entire toilet set was kept on the aptly named washstand, a piece of furniture that matched the balance of the furniture in the bedroom. If a person was careless when getting his bath in the morning, water could be splashed on the wallpaper behind the washstand. For that reason the furniture makers put a frame on either side with a rod through it. A large towel was made to be used on it to prevent the water from splashing on the wallpaper, hence the name splasher. Most of the large, fancy towels found today were made for this purpose. One of the reasons so many splashers will still be found today is the fact bathrooms were few and far between in the rural areas until about the middle of this century. The people in those areas continued to use their bowls and pitchers on the washstands, and as long as they used them they needed and made splashers.

They also made towels of all kinds and sizes, everything from the most acceptable fifteen by twenty seven inch size to the smaller "finger" towel size which was about nine inches wide. One early article suggested that "small embroidered towels are always welcome gifts, since every bathroom needs a plentiful supply of these small linens for guests purposes, and a flock of them on the towel bars adds a very festive touch of color." Hardly a month passed that some magazine didn't have a page on towels or towel patterns. They were touted as the perfect gift, or as some suggested "several embroidered towels make an excellent gift." An article in a 1921 *Needlecraft Magazine* began with "Truly, 'Every homemaker loves a towel', whether she is the mistress of a mansion, a cottage, an apartment, or a single room which she calls home, especially if that very useful bit of household linen is daintily decorated with lace or embroidery, or both. Hence we givers of good gifts can make no mis-

take in adding to our Christmas-boxes a generous supply of towels. The decoration may be simple or elaborate; it is the touch of "real handwork" that adds charm and distinction." The article was published in January so as to give the women ample time to make the illustrated towels to add to their Christmas boxes for the coming December. There were several things in the articles that would inspire the average towel maker. For example, if the mistress of a mansion would appreciate towels, then surely her family and friends would as well. And if a bit of "handwork" would add so much charm and distinction, she was delighted to do it.

One of the reasons that towels were so highly touted as the perfect gift could be the fact they were so inexpensive and so easy to make. Huck and plain linen weaves seemed to be the fabric of choice, and only a small amount of embroidery thread and crochet cotton was needed. The towel might only have one initial or there could be two or three. Even if the maker wanted to add lace, only fifteen inches or less of crochet, knitted, or tatted lace was required. And it could be wide or narrow. Some of the towels were much more elaborate as some had drawn work while others had wide bands of handmade lace insertion. Apparently towels were made by the hundreds, and one of the reasons we can find so many today could be the fact that writers suggested, as one did in 1939, that "We are learning to delight in cheerful bathrooms, and a bit of brightness in the form of a prettily decorated hand-wipe [towel, probably finger size] is a great addition, even though it should not often be called into real service—other than as a dress-up." The article began with "They are sure of the heartiest sort of welcome, of course, not alone because everybody loves a pretty towel, but because it is such a pleasure to work on them—making them ready for the gift box, an engagement shower, or to bestow a special touch of glory on your own towel rack."

With this constant reminder of how well towels were accepted, how much everybody loved them, and instructions for making new designs being given almost monthly in one magazine or another, it is small wonder that so many were made. And after seeing all that praise for needlework, something the women were already doing, and the discussions about the joys of sharing it is even easier to understand why so many pieces of needlework, especially towels, are still available today. And they are available in a wide range of sizes and types of needlework now. Generally linen dealers will have about twice as many towels as any other pieces. The good news is that towel prices are still quite reasonable. Of course the smaller ones with only a small amount of work will be priced much less than a large splasher with lots of drawnwork and maybe a monogram.

Splasher with crocheted lace insertion at either end as well as on the bottom. Letter K embroidered in blue. $11-$16.

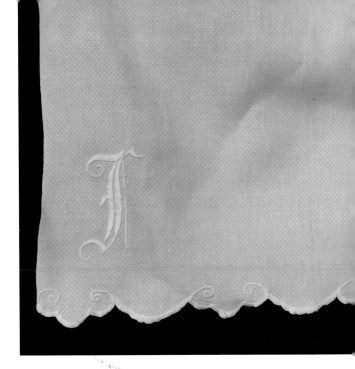

Mongrams are usually in the center of the towel. On this one it is on one side. $8-$11.

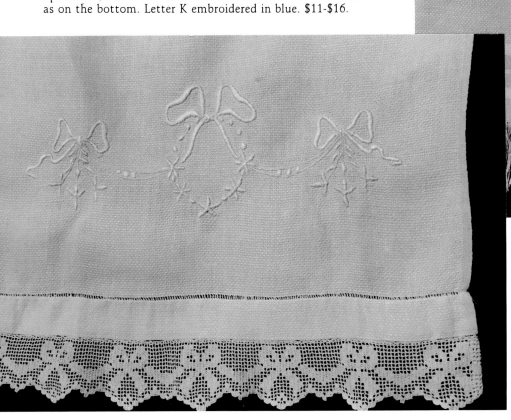

Towel with woven stripes, embroidery, and fringe. $9-$11.

Crocheted lace and embroidery decorate this towel. $9-$11.

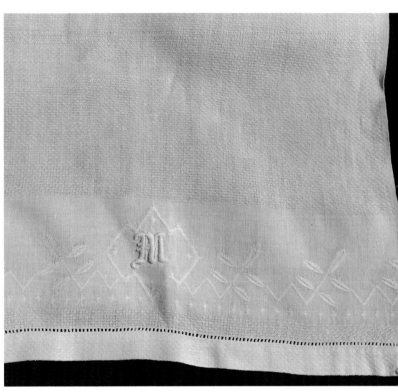

Terry cloth hand and bath towels with tatted lace. $10-$14.

Towel with hemstitched hem and monogram. $8-$13.

Towels like this with the same design on either side, in different colors, are quite popular. $21-$28.

During the past few years towels with colored, especially red, designs woven in have become extremely popular. Hand tied fringe seems to have helped the popularity. Prices have risen accordingly. $19-$26.

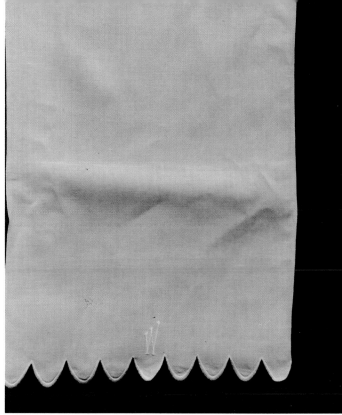

Red stripe on this one is rather narrow but the drawn work and triple-tied long fringe makes it very collectible. $22-$29.

Attractive towel with lots of needlework. $10-$14.

This towel was undoubtedly made to commemorate some special event on Columbus Day. $20-$27.

Towel made of crash fabric with tatted insertion and border. Two rows of drawn work. $14-$18.

Satin stitched design outlined in yellow. $12-$16.

Monogrammed towel with crocheted lace. $9-$13.

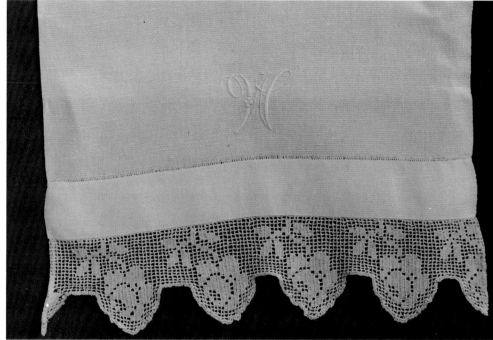

Monogrammed towel with crocheted lace. $12-$15.

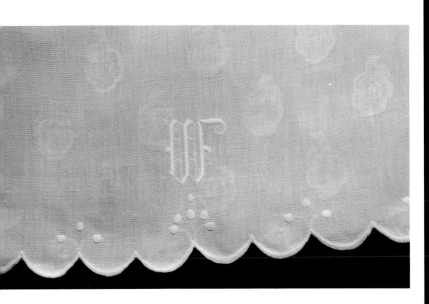

Monogrammed towel with scalloped edge. $8-$14.

Towel with one-letter monogram and crocheted lace. $10-$13.

Small towel with letter T done in tiny cross stitches. $6-$8.

Hemstitched and monogrammed towel. $9-$13.

Towel with lace insertion. $9-$13.

Splasher with drawn work on either end. $17-$20.

Towel with three-letter monogram. $10-$14.

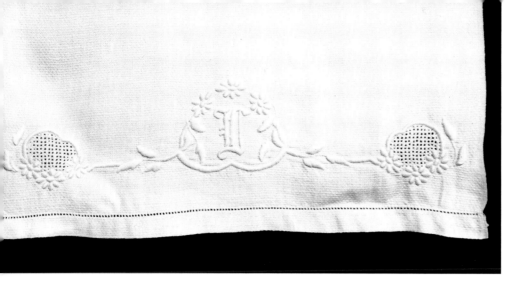

Towel with lots of needlework. $11-$14.

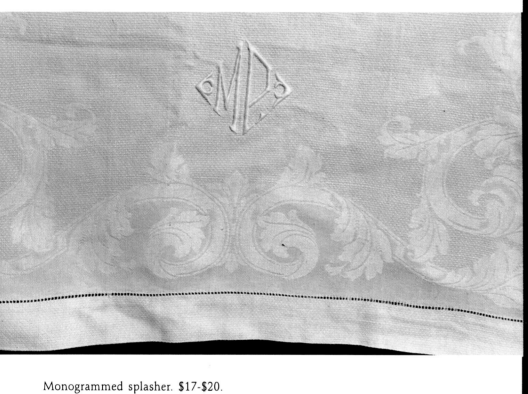

Monogrammed splasher. $17-$20.

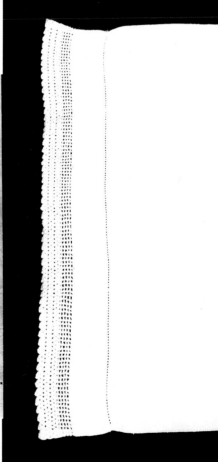

Towel with wide crocheted lace. $10-$13.

Monogrammed towel with scalloped bottom. $14-$17.

124

Monogrammed single letter splasher. $18-$24.

Splasher with simple white-on-white embroidery. $14-$19.

Towel with three-letter monogram and crocheted lace insertion. $16-$19.

Towel with letter G in filet crocheted diamond. $7-$9.

Tatted lace and a simple monogram were used on this towel. $12-$15.

Towel with simple cross stitch monogram. $7-$9.

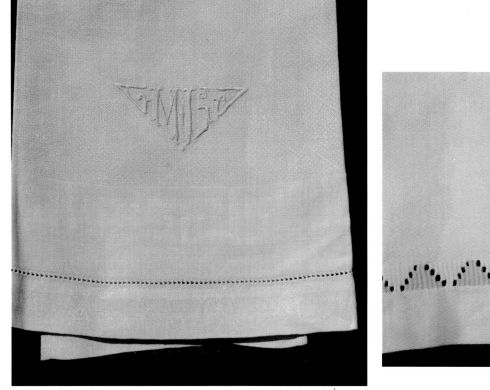

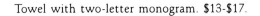

Towel with two-letter monogram. $13-$17.

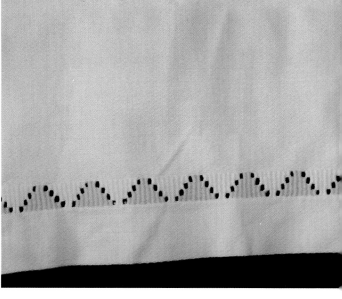

Swedish weaving or embroidery was a favorite form of decoration for towels. $10-$14.

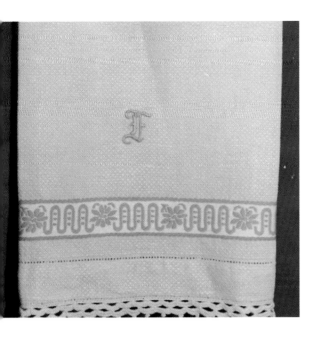

Towel with embroidered yellow band, initial, and crocheted lace. $13-$17.

Beige splasher with lace crocheted in a lighter shade of beige. $19-$24.

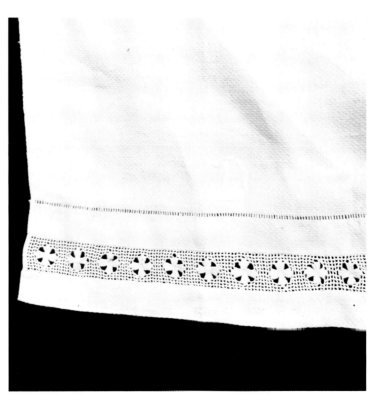

Towels and dresser scarves were often made to match. $13-$17

Towel with crocheted insertion. $12-$16.

Small towel with letter F in small wreath, crocheted lace. $15-$19.

Towel with three-letter monogram in red. $8-$11.

Three towels.

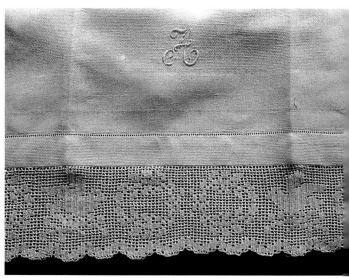

Splasher with wide crocheted lace. $20-$23.

Three different towels

Splasher with hand-tied fringe. $19-$27.

Fringed splasher. $17-$24.

Monogrammed towel with fringe. $10-$14.

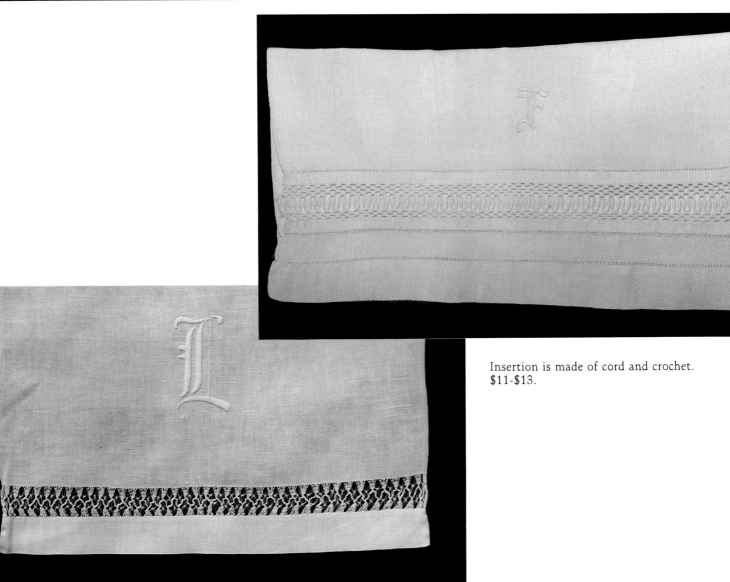

Insertion is made of cord and crochet. $11-$13.

Linen splasher with drawn work and monogram. $16-$23.

Plain towel with simple embroidery. $8-$11.

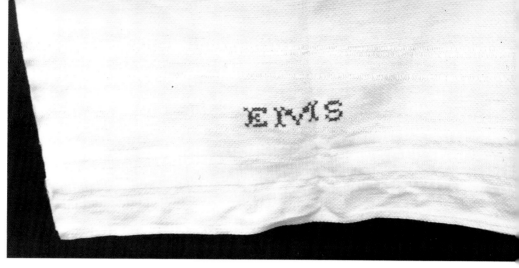

Plain splasher with single letter S. $11-$15.

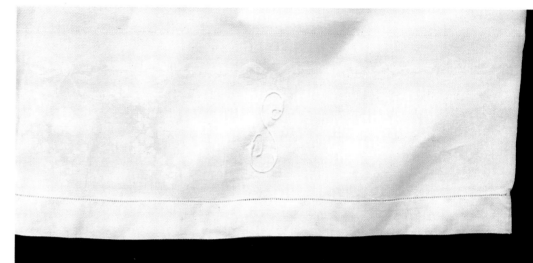

Plain towel. $7-$9.

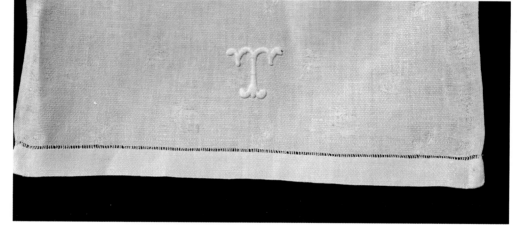

Linen towel was apparently made more for show than use. Much needlework, but linen absorbs water too easily. $15-$18.

Plain splasher. $19-$13.

Towel with embroidered design and scalloped border. $11-
$14.

Dainty towel, embroidered daisies, tatted lace. $13-$15.

Towel with net type lace and fringe.
$17-$19.

132

Chapter Twelve
Tray and Teacart Cloths

It is easy to understand how the breakfast tray became so popular about half to a century or more ago. People did not go to the hospital then as hospitals were small, compared to the present ones, and not only were they small, usually only the rich and the very sick were admitted. Invalids and the chronically ill were cared for by the family—at home. In fact, illnesses were such an accepted fact of life that my mountaineer aunt who could cure nearly any ailment with herbs insisted no one should ever go to a doctor except for broken bones and gunshot wounds. The sick were kept at home and nursed back to health. Women had their babies at home, and it was the custom for them to stay in bed for a week or so after the birth. Of course the sick had to eat so food was taken to the bed on a tray, generally called a breakfast tray. This type of tray was so popular and so widely used, that the one used by President Franklin D. Roosevelt is in the museum at his Little White House estate in Warm Springs, Georgia. Newspapers were always a part of the breakfast tray, and the one in the tray at Warm Springs was the one published on the day he died.

It was essential that the food be served attractively as this encouraged the sick person to eat whether they were hungry or not. Since this was the time when all types of household linens were being made in profusion, it was only natural that cloths, both simple and ornate, be made for the breakfast or meal tray. And if it was being made, then there were articles about them in some of the needlecraft magazines. One such article appeared in the August 1927 issue of *Needlecraft Magazine*. The author, a Ms. Guppy, explained how "This little set of three pieces—the oblong twelve by eighteen inches, the napkins twelve inches square, fills a long-felt need, and may be kept for the sole purpose of individual tray-meals. Indeed, the breakfast or luncheon set for the entire family may be easily evolved from it, since the tray cover is of just the right size for the placemat or serviette, and the centerpiece may be made square, with the same decoration on each side; or the three pieces may serve as a buffet set. Let us be sure, however, to provide this lovely set for our sometime invalid, and keep it tucked away in readiness for possible need." In the February 1928 issue of the same magazine another writer discussed the advantages and uses of the three piece set this way: "While the claim of novelty can no longer be advanced, the popularity which was attained by the three-piece set at the beginning of its career is as persistent as ever and its vogue undisputed. To the greatest extent it has taken the place of the scarf for the buffet or bureau. Not only does it serve the purpose of the allover cover in protecting the polished wood—it is far more decora-

tive, and this means a great deal to the woman who finds her chief pleasure in promoting the beauty and cheer of her home. Again, it spells unity in various ways; it may serve as an individual breakfast set, or take its place on milady's dressing table as one of the newer vanity sets. And the pieces may be used separately for tray covers, doilies, or wherever there is need."

This information will probably have a startling effect on many linen collectors because it again proves how nearly impossible it is to classify any specific category without fear of contradiction. About the only way to be absolutely positive regarding the way a piece was used originally, or what purpose it was made for, is when it has remained in the family where someone remembers how it was used. And this may not be absolutely correct because as the early writers have stressed, the same piece or pieces could have been used in many different ways. We have always been inclined to call the three piece sets vanity sets because the vanity was very popular in our childhood. In the thirties and forties all the women in our neighborhood were very busy making vanity sets for the vanity that was part of the new bedroom set. At that time so many people were disposing of the heavy old oak furniture they had used since the very early part of the century. Perhaps the reason it is so difficult to sort out all these pieces is the fact no napkins have been found that match the pieces we have always identified as tray cloths. But when it was discovered that three piece sets could and were used not only as tray cloths, but as sets for the buffet, bureau, and vanity, identification was no longer easy. To add to the confusion three piece antimassacar sets were made about this time for use on chairs. Some of these later ones were embroidered on fabric just like the other sets. They usually had some kind of lady with a hat design which helps some because most of the older ones had floral, animal, or perhaps a house design.

Unless you are a real connoisseur of household linens there is still another one that can be confused with the tray cloth—the teacart or tea wagon cloth. It is about the same size as some of the other cloths, and will have similar designs, but napkins were never made with this cloth. Since so many napkins have been lost through the years, that doesn't help much in the identification department, yet it does keep the collector from searching for matching napkins, especially when the cloth is known to have been made for teacart use. It is believed the teacart began its reign of popularity during the height of the social custom of tea time. The cart was used to bring and keep extra refreshments and beverages near the tea table. Even if the hostess had a maid, the cart was very useful because the maid could bring additional

133

refreshments and the hostess did not have to leave her guests to go to the kitchen. But in this era of beautifully done household linens it would have been unthinkable to use the teacart without a lavishly done cloth. This use presented a close-up look at the hostess' needlework and evoked the praise of her peers.

We have learned through the trial and error method that so many household linens can be used today to fit our modern needs, but these tray and teacart cloths were used in so many ways originally it is going to be very difficult to find new ways to use them. But we are willing to bet that someone will. In fact, we have just thought of one that might work—framing a particularly ornate one to make a wall decoration.

Cheerful tray cloth probably used for serving the sick and the invalids. $19-$24.

Same cloth shown on breakfast tray.

In some cases place mats served a dual role. They could be used on the table or a tray. $5-$7.

Unusual design for tray cloth, could have been made for child's tray. $12-$15.

Close-up of the frog in the center.

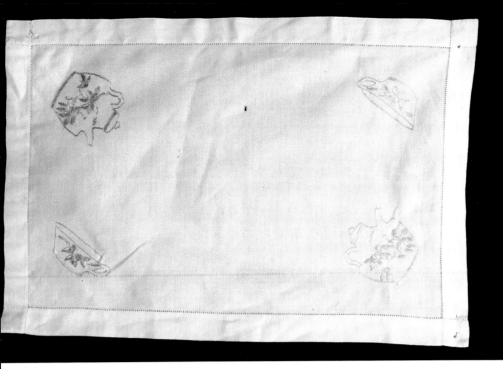

Tea cart cloth with pots and cups embroidered in gold silk thread. $15-$18.

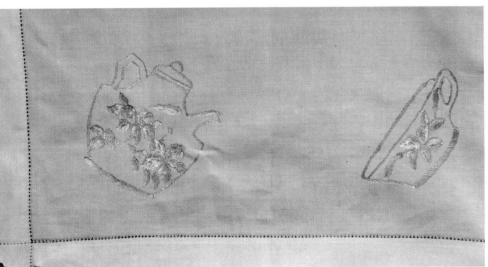

Close-up of one end of cloth.

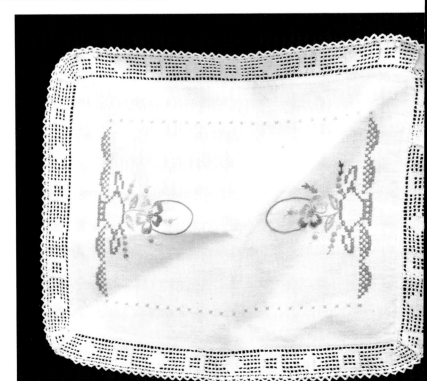

Colored embroidery on tray cloth. One of few with lace. $10-$14.

Fringed cloth for tray or tea cart. $11-$14.

Miniature and full size chafing dishes on tea cart. Turkey red embroidered flowers and leaves are on the cloth. $15-$18.

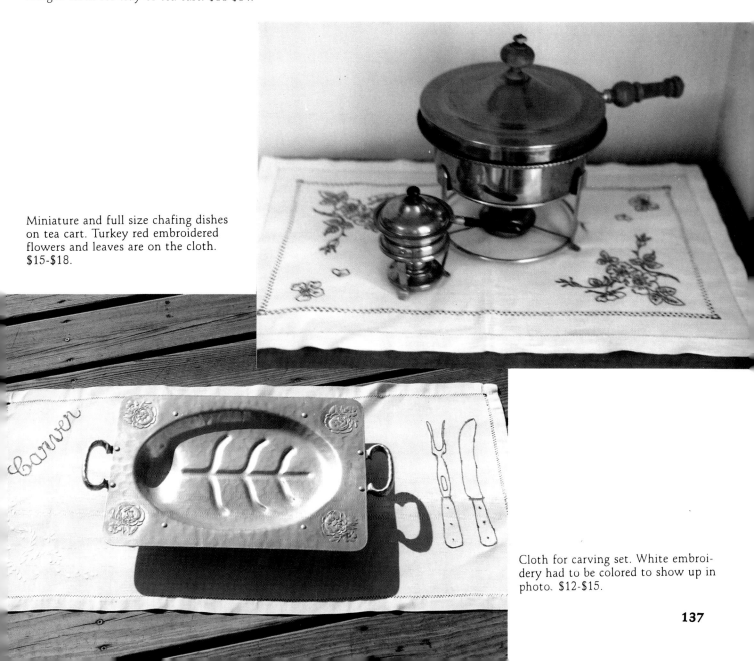

Cloth for carving set. White embroidery had to be colored to show up in photo. $12-$15.

137

Breakfast tray with fringed cloth done in gold thread and drawn work. $15-$18.

Another turkey red embroidered cloth on tea cart. Copper coffee service, $15-$18.

Two rows of drawn work on plain cloth. $9-$14.

Cloth with knife, fork, and spoon plus vegetables embroidered in turkey red. Fringe worn. $13-$15, perfect $18-$22.

Tray cloth with knife, fork, and spoon embroidered in red. $13-$16.

Extra wide cloth was made to cover the drop leaves on tea carts when they were raised. $22-$27.

Place mat also used as tray cloth. Bright embroidery. $5-$9.

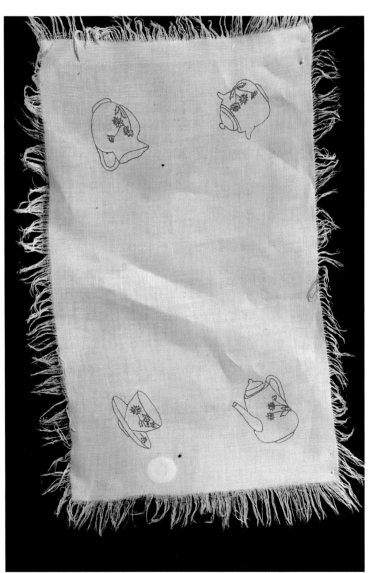

Tea cart cloth with pot, creamer, sugar dish, cup and saucer embroidered in red. $15-$17.

Fringed cloth embroidered in red. $14-$17.

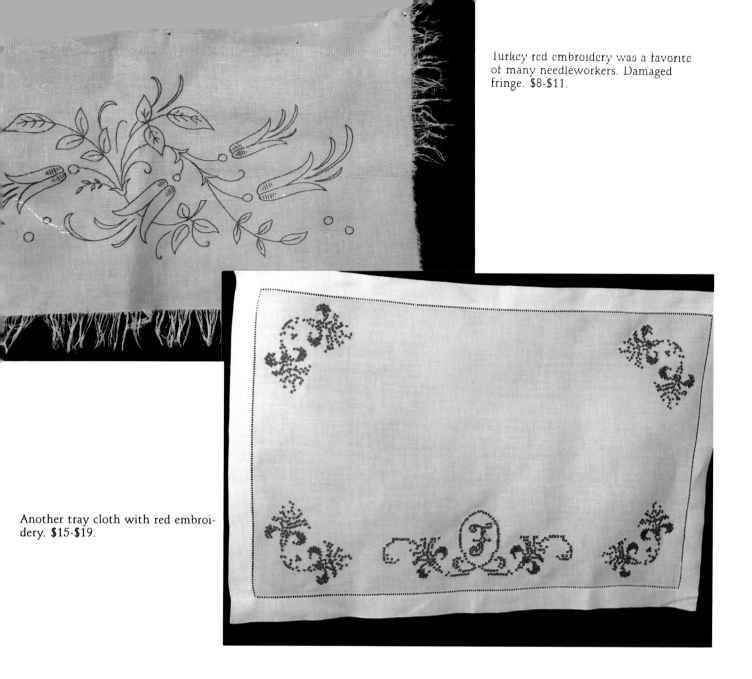

Turkey red embroidery was a favorite of many needleworkers. Damaged fringe. $8-$11.

Another tray cloth with red embroidery. $15-$19.

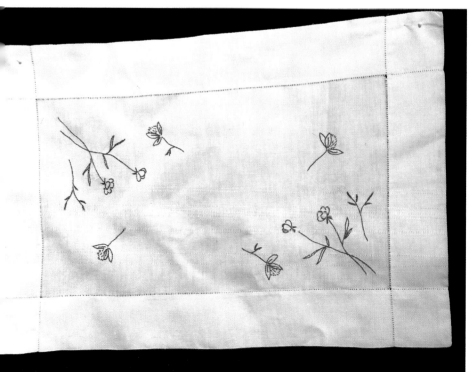

Tray cloth with wide hem and tiny red flowers. $13-$16.

Tray cloth, more red embroidery. $16-$19.

Tray cloth with embroidered flowers. $13-$17.

Similiar to cloth above but different design. $13-$17.

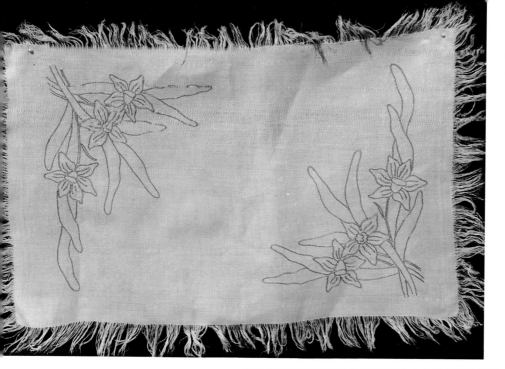

Cloth embroidered with gold flowers. $17-$20.

Tray cloth similar to one above. $16-$19.

Tray with red embroidery. $15-$17.

143

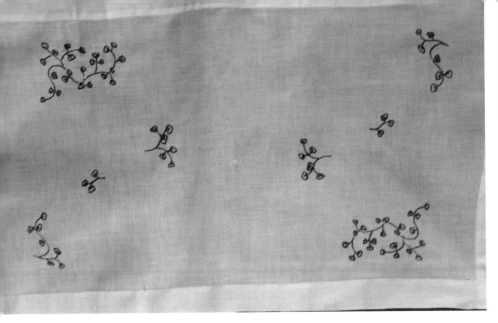

Tray cloth with yet another red design. $14-$17.

Canton linen tray cloth probably made in China or the Philippines in the forties. $13-$16.

Tray cloth with embroidery in brown. Hand tied fringe on either end. $17-$19.

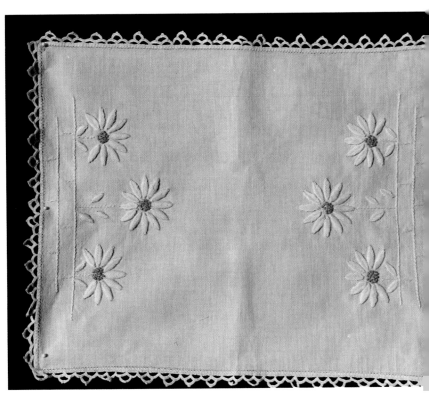

Tray cloth with embroidered daisies and crocheted lace. $12-$15.

Fringed tray cloth. $12-$15.

Cross stitched cloth that could double as place mat or tray cloth. $7-$9.

Tray cloth with poor quality drawn work and good embroidery. $18-$21.

Chapter Thirteen
Caring for Old Linens

Several factors are involved in caring for old linens which have to be resolved before any decisions on the care can be made. The three most important factors are the type of fabric, condition, and approximate age. If it is a good, strong type linen in reasonably good condition, chances are it can be washed with the regular household linens. But even in cases like this one must use caution. A decade or so ago I bought a cross stitched, linen tablecloth, the stamped kind Bucilla was famous for selling in the 1940s. It was in excellent condition except for a light brown circle about eight to ten inches in diameter. It seemed natural to assume the stain had been caused by something like coffee that had not been washed out right away. The dealer and I discussed the various ways the stain could be removed. Since I had had good luck with the cold water/hot water method, I started with it. The part of the cloth with the circle was placed over a bowl and cold water was allowed to run through it. The stain did seem to lighten some, but I know now it was the fabric deteriorating. Feeling quite smug about my good luck in removing the spot, I turned on the hot water so it could run through the cloth. In seconds there was nothing left of the spot as the fabric had completely dissolved leaving a large, round, gaping hole. Whatever caused the stain had caused the fabric to rot. This doesn't happen too often, but collectors should be aware that it can happen. For this reason one should not pay big prices for pieces with damage or stains as they may be harder to fix than you think. Our ancestors were a frugal lot and they would have probably patched the hole in the tablecloth. Having found quite a few pieces of household linens that were patched, I know this method was not uncommon in the early days. There was and still is so much work on the handmade household linens it seems a crying shame not to use them just as long as possible. I wasn't quite that frugal, but I did salvage enough fabric out of the tablecloth to make a number of lampshades. The good fabric and the beautiful needlework was salvaged and used to an advantage.

As we can see by the above the age of the fabric is not an all-determining factor. A lot depends on how it has been used and cared for through the years. Those of us who still do needlework today are very careful about laundering those pieces, but apparently it was a different story fifty years or so ago. We do know that needleworkers at that time sold a lot of their work to people who either would not or could not do fancy stitchery. This meant they only had money invested, not time, money, and labor; therefore they were not nearly as careful with their handmade linens as the maker might have been because so many pieces could

be found several years ago with the commercial laundry tags still stapled in the corner. Care has to be used in removing those tags or the fabric will be torn. The best way to remove those tags seems to be with a fruit knife. The blade is used to raised the folded-over ends which in turn allows the metal tags to be removed. Although the fabric was probably new when the pieces were first sent to the commercial laundry, it behooves us to now use greater care when cleaning those pieces.

A great place to find directions or advice on caring for old linens is in the old needlework magazines. These magazines will often be found at antique malls and flea markets priced in the $3 to $5 each range. Most of the advice they gave then was for new pieces of needlework, nevertheless it can still be used today, maybe sometimes with slight variations.

The chances of finding large boxes of old household linens at one time are not nearly as likely today as they were a couple of decades ago. But they can still be found at some auctions and estate sales. Then there are people like the lady in our area who had a yard sale about every other weekend for an entire summer. At each sale she offered a large, new box of linens, some good, some bad, and some mediocre. They were priced by the piece which allowed early arrivals to pick and choose. Prices were good, but there was one catch that wasn't too noticeable out in the yard, and that was the fact she and her husband were heavy cigarette smokers. The linens I bought at her sales have been washed often during the past 7 or 8 years, yet they still have a slight tobacco odor. So, if you are allergic to certain odors, you might want to watch for them as linens that have been packed away for years will have odors—everything from mold (musty) to tobacco.

When buying linens that are slightly dirty, or yellowed, it is always a good idea to check the fabric for strength before beginning the cleaning process. You want to know if it is still strong or has it become weakened through the years. A good test for this is to pull the fabric ever so gently while holding it between the thumb and forefinger. It will be easy then to tell whether it is still strong—or if it has been weakened by years of wear and tear not to mention laundering. Another test is to hold the fabric to the light so you can check the threads in the folds. Threads will begin to break in fabric that has been folded the same way too long, or if it has been exposed to sunlight too much. It is always a good idea to fold your old linens a different way each time they are laundered.

Each person has to make the decision about how they want to clean and preserve their old household linens. That knowledge will come with experience; therefore our suggestion for new collectors is to start with the less expensive pieces—just in case something goes wrong. You get the feel after a short time, and you can almost predict which methods will work best. But it is always a good idea to start with a very gentle cleaning process. Since the majority of old linens found today will only be yellowed from being packed away too long, or just have some dirt or dust accumulation, we have found the easiest and best way to clean them is to soak them overnight in a bathtub full of cold water. The linens can be removed in the morning (a few pieces at a time if there is a large collection) and put in a sink full of warm water and mild soap. It has been found that it is better to swish the linens through the water rather than rub or squeeze them, unless absolutely necessary. Quilts can also be washed this way, but due to their size it is best to remove the cold water and finish the cleaning process in the bathtub. You won't have to worry about the initial cleaning, if the linens are bought from a reputable linen dealer as they will already be clean. But you might want to ask her what method she used so you can continue with one that works.

All the old needlework magazines suggested the use of Ivory soap for washing one's fine linens. They also suggested using spring water. With so many chemicals in our water supply today, we have found it advantageous to buy spring water to wash our very finest linens. We have also found that when the mild soap doesn't remove the dirt or the yellow, a few drops of Woolite added to the water helps tremendously. After the linens have been washed, they should be rinsed two to three times in fresh water. And you never want to use real hot water as it is felt it will harm the fabric or the embroidery thread, especially on the pieces embroidered with silk thread. One of the interesting things about the advice given in the old magazines for caring for linens was the fact it was put into language anyone could understand. An example is the advice to only use warm water when washing newly embroidered pieces. So one could understand just how warm, they described it this way, "not quite as warm as the hand can bear."

Pieces done with silk embroidery thread are not as plentiful as they were a few years ago. Perhaps this is due to the fact one has to be super careful when washing and ironing those pieces. Apparently using silk thread for all types of needlework was very popular about a century ago as we have found one 60-page catalog from The Eureka Silk Manufacturing Company with outlets in Boston, New York, Chicago, and St. Louis. They gave instructions for making all types of clothing and household linens, but no directions for caring for them. It is doubtful anyone ever looked for directions for linen care in catalogs as all the magazines of that era had at least one page devoted to their care. They suggested that you wash all the pieces embroidered in silk separately, and in "earthernware bowls" as opposed to sinks and tubs. More patience was required in caring for linens done with silk thread than with linen or cotton thread. The consensus of opinion among the experts was that linens embroidered with cotton or linen thread should be placed

between two towels and spread flat until they were dry, but it was okay to roll the towels holding the pieces embroidered with silk thread. The reason for this, they said, was the fact the silk thread had to be perfectly dry as damp thread produced steam that could and would take the life out of the silk leaving it dull and lusterless. If the center became too dry, a damp cloth could be placed over it while it was ironed. We still use this old method because we suspect the use of a steam iron would have the same effect on the piece as that generating from the damp thread.

For fifty years, from around 1880 to about 1930, the choice for skilled needleworkers was white-on-white, that is white embroidery on white fabric. Some of the most beautiful linens made during the past century are the white-on-whites. As they age they are also the hardest to keep snowy white. A couple of tips picked up from older relatives on keeping them white still works for us, and both are easy. Use about a fourth cup of vinegar in a sink full of rinse water, and it will works wonders in the whitening department. Spreading freshly washed linens on the grass in bright sunlight also helps to keep them white. Stronger chemicals, commercial cleaners, and whiteners can also be used, but they should only be used after they have been tested on linens the owner is willing to lose—if worst comes to worst. Some will work on some fabrics, others on different fabrics, and then there are those that will completely destroy the fabric. An example of this hearsay advice happened to us a decade or so ago. A linen dealer who did some of the big antique shows in the northeast kept a group in a mall enthralled while she told us how stupid we were to wash our linens so carefully. She said she simply threw all of her linens, regardless of the type of fabric, in the washing machine with a cup of dishwashing detergent and a couple of cups of liquid detergent. We should have known better, but she sounded so convincing we returned home and fortunately only tried a small load of poor quality linens. All we got for our efforts was a clogged washing machine as the fabric had all disintegrated. There wasn't a piece left that was large enough to identify any of the linens. We decided at that time that each person would have to make their own decisions about using stronger cleaners

Ironing linens can be even more tedious than washing them. First, the ironing board has to be well padded, and several extra cloths are necessary for use over and under the pieces. Embroidered pieces should be ironed first on the top side and then on the opposite or back side. This makes the embroidery stand out. As you continue to collect and use your linens there are many little tricks you will learn that will work best for you, and will make the caring process easier.

One thing is absolutely essential. When and if you decide to sell your linens, wash and iron them carefully before offering them for sale. Not only will you get a better price, but they will sell better. Nothing turns off a linen buyer like a pile of dirty, dingy linens, no matter how good they are.

Chapter Fourteen
More Uses for Damaged Linens

Once upon a time, not too long ago, women carried umbrellas or parasols to keep their complexions as fair as possible. Unlike today, when a tan is very fashionable, in those days a light complexion was equally as desirable. Both women and girls wore big floppy hats while working in the garden or among the flowers. Farm girls wore bonnets made especially to shield them from the sun. But when they went out in public it was another matter. They always carried a parasol. In the early days they often made their own parasol covers, that is, they generally embroidered a cover to put on their frame. They might make the cover and the lace to go around the border, or they might just embroider a cover. Instructions for making the covers were given in many of the needlecraft magazines. Today parasols are carried to protect the owner from rain, and nobody would think of taking a fancy embroidered one out in the rain. Another reason the old ones would not be used is the fact so few of them can still be found, and when found the price is usually completely out of reason, or the fabric is damaged.

But don't despair! Help is on the way, and you don't even need damaged linens to achieve your goal. In fact, you don't even need an old parasol, although they are more attractive. All you need to make a very attractive parasol is a round, embroidered centerpiece, or you can use a crocheted, tatted, or knitted one provided you can find one that looks good on your parasol. Generally a black parasol is used because the needlework shows up better on it, but other colors can be equally attractive. All that is left is tacking the centerpiece at intervals around the parasol after centering the needlework exactly on the top. Then since you won't likely be using it while out for a stroll, it has been found the next best use is to leave it open (to show off the top) and place it in a corner of the room, on a shelf or maybe a table in the corner.

There was a time when small, crocheted medallions, the type used to make bedspreads and tablecloths, could be found in large quantities and at cheap prices in sewing baskets and old trunks at estate sales. They were generally bought by people who planned to use them in making clothes for their dolls. Now lots of people are searching for them and they are no longer found in sewing baskets or trunks. Linen dealers have found how popular they can be with the many new uses that have been devised through the years. Now similar pieces will generally be found packaged in small plastic bags with prices tags larger than those formerly found on a entire sewing baskets full. But as we all know, supply and demand governs all prices, and today the supply is small and the demand large.

You can get lucky and find stacks of small crocheted pieces selling for around 25 cents each. So much can be done with these small pieces. They can be sewn on tee shirts to make a very attractive design. Or they can be fastened with pins on Styrofoam balls to make attractive Christmas decorations, either for the tree or to use on the mantel. Use you own imagination when creating the design, but old beads, torn apart or left on the string, can add much to the design. Oftentimes small lace, handmade and factory-made, squares will be seen. They can be tacked on knitting bags to add a personal touch. One woman we know has made a shoulder bag as well as a knitting bag out of denim—to use when she wears her jeans. She has added a piece of lace or crochet to each for a touch of individuality.

Lamp shades made out of damaged linens—anything from bedspreads and coverlets to tablecloths—are extra bonuses when you have a fine old piece like the pink luster pitcher. The lid of the pitcher was broken and the bedspread badly damaged. By combining the two and using pink ribbon to tie them together, we ended up with a beautiful lamp. There are many other things just begging to be use. Let your imagination run wild and see what you can salvage.

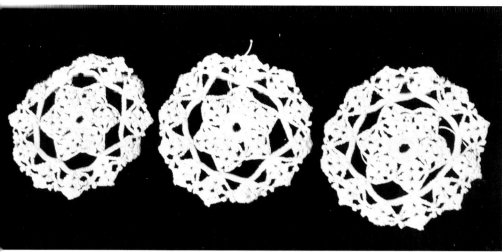

Odd pieces of crochet like this are cheap and can be used in numerous ways.

These satin Christmas balls were decorated with odds and ends of crochet, tatting, and beading.

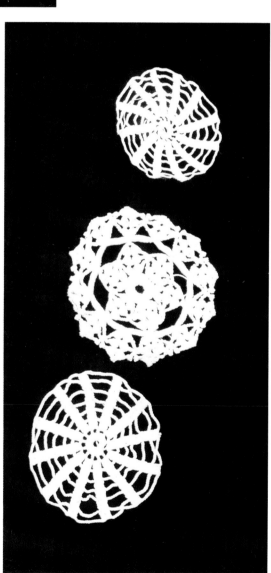

Different designs but can be used as easily.

An odd piece of lace tacked on a knitting bag makes it special, whether as a gift or for the maker.

Victorian ladies embroidered their parasol covers. Now similar results can be obtained with much less work. Simply tack an embroidered centerpiece on a new or old parasol.

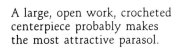

A large, open work, crocheted centerpiece probably makes the most attractive parasol.

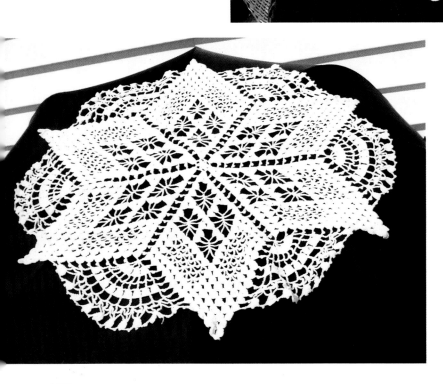

A different crocheted centerpiece changes the appearance altogether.

Even Battenberg centerpieces can be used on parasols.

The crazy quilt idea was used to make this Christmas stocking out of velvet scraps. Lace was removed from another damaged piece.

A red and white crocheted centerpiece makes a new parasol out of this old black one.

Odds and ends of needlework along with old post cards make Christmas packages more attractive.

Battenberg scarf on mantle with homemade Christmas decorations is especially attractive.

Damaged bedspreads can be used to make lamp shades. In this case pink ribbon was used because the lamp had been made out of a pink luster teapot whose lid had been shattered.

Chapter Fifteen
Miscellaneous

Again there are the leftovers, not enough to fill a category, yet too important not to use. Topping the list are antimacassars and chair backs that were so popular up until about half a century ago, and now surprisingly seem to be returning to favor among a few homemakers—in a limited way. Antimacassars, as some of you may remember, were the three-piece chair sets made originally to protect the back of the chair from the grease or oil that rubbed off the men's heads. In the mountains they used bear grease to hold their hair in place when they went courting; in other areas it was oil or tonic, but it would all rub off and ruin the back of the chair. So, the women solved that problem by making antimacassars and chair backs that could be washed, ironed, and returned to the chair. In time some of the antimacassars were reduced to one piece, the so-called chair back that only covered the top of the chair. The pieces made for the arms were used primarily to protect them from dirty hands. Somewhere along the way apparently the women had convinced the men to wash their hands before sitting in the good chairs which meant those pieces were no longer needed. Like all the other household linen designs, the women used familiar things such as animals, flowers, or even a house with Home Sweet Home done in filet crochet for decoration. Not all the antimacassars were crocheted, in fact some were knitted while a limited number were tatted. Then there were a few that were made of fabric, usually linen, with an embroidered design.

Although the custom of entertaining one's friends at tea time was long considered the property of the rich and socially correct; nevertheless many wannabes tried their hand at mastering the ritual. The difference can be seen today in the linens they made and used. Those who could afford it had beautifully done linens, either ones they had made themselves or had had made by expert needleworkers. The lace on the cloths was wide and perfectly executed whereas the lace on the others was usually factory made, and the designs plainer. An example of the later is the small sugar and creamer doily.

Women who crocheted seemed to make more novelties than those who knitted and tatted. Maybe it was the fact crochet adapted better to these projects. Whatever the reason more novelties will be found in crochet than in other needlework. The small cups and saucers in the illustrations are an example.

Christmas has always been the time when needleworkers could show off their work to the best advantage. They could and did make exquisite linens for the beds, tables, and chairs, but they seem to enjoy most making things with which to decorate their homes for the holidays. One of those special things was the stockings, both large and small. The large ones could be hung on the mantel while the smaller ones went on the tree. They may be done in petit point or any other type of needlework, but they are always welcome, either by the family or as gifts for friends.

Needleworkers are also known to have made a wide variety of Christmas stockings. $5-$7.

Needleworkers, like basketmakers, enjoy varying their work. One of them crocheted dozens of these novelty cups and saucers. $3-$4.

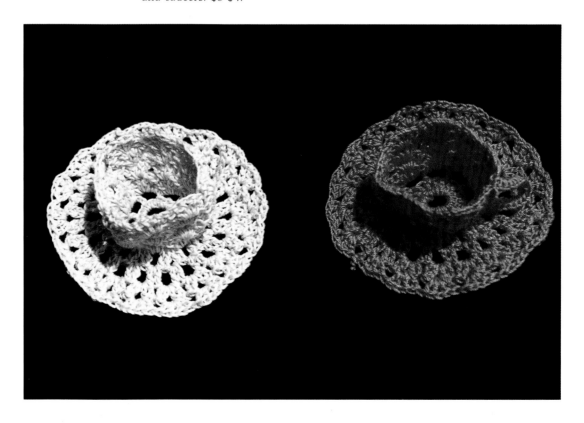

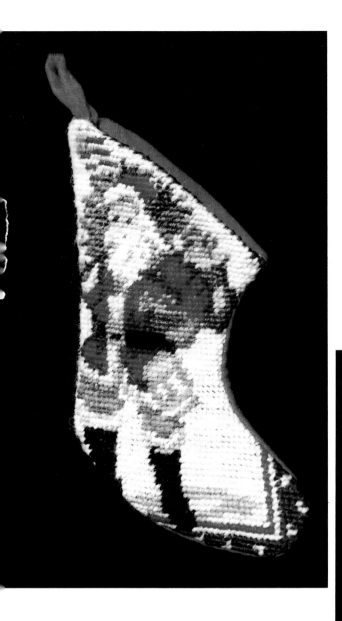

Small needlepoint and petit point stocking made to be hung on the tree. $10-$14.

This is another of those pieces where only the maker knew its real use. It could have been anything from a different type centerpiece to a covering for a hat. $15-$20.

Cross stitched cloth for sugar dish and creamer. $7-$9.

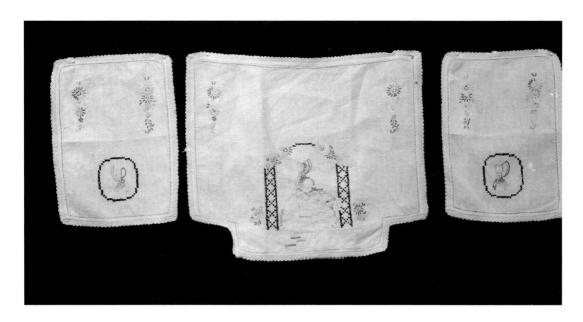

Antimacassar sets were also embroidered. $13-$17.

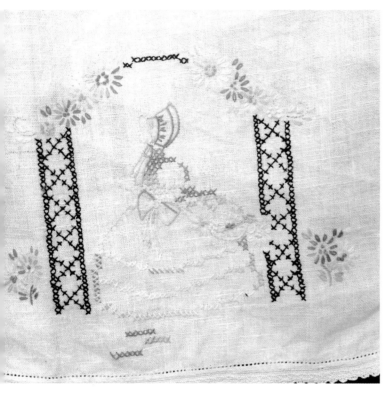

Close-up of the embroidery.

Ninety something woman remembers making this chenille bedspread for a child's bed, in the fifties. $20-$30.

156

Filet crocheted chair back. $15-$20.

Antimacassar sets were different than chair backs because
they had matching pieces for the arms. $20-$25.

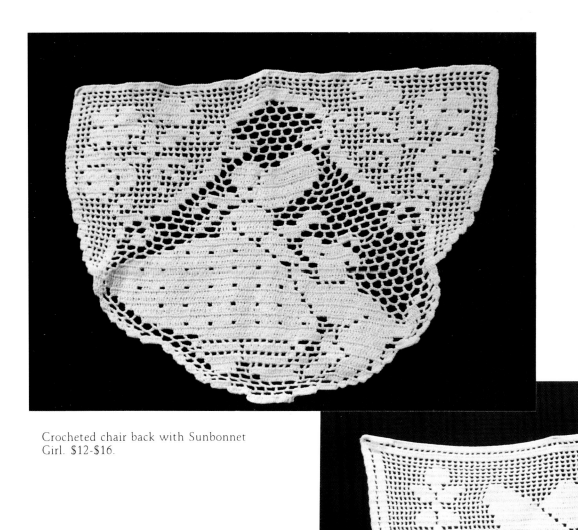

Crocheted chair back with Sunbonnet
Girl. $12-$16.

Circa 1930-40 crocheted chair back. $13-$17.

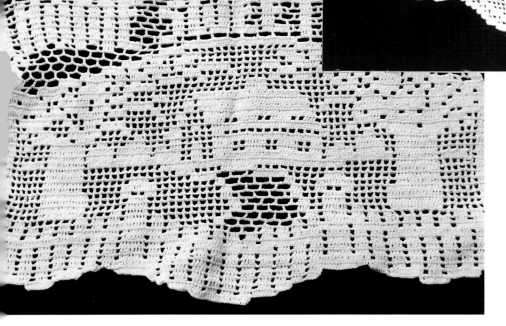

Crocheted chair backs lost much of
their popularity during the last half
century, but they do seem to have
gained some of it back in recent years.
$15-$20.